THE

GREAT

POTATO

B O O K

THE
GREAT
POTATO
BOOK

Florence Fabricant

FOREWORD BY CHARLIE TROTTER

PHOTOGRAPHY BY RICHARD BLAIR

TEN SPEED PRESS

BERKELEY   TORONTO

CONTENTS

Acknowledgments

Like devising and preparing a menu, writing a book involves the layering and interaction of many ingredients: the individuals and organizations who lend their support to bring the project to the table, so to speak.

Those who deserve special thanks, and an extra helping of buttery mashed potatoes, are Kirsty Melville, whose appetite was tempted by this colorful subject; Holly Taines White, who monitored it, nudged her author along, vetted every word, and was more forgiving than most editors when it came to deadlines; Rick Bishop of Mountain Sweet Berry Farm, who, on a stormy autumn day many years ago in the company of David Bouley, Joël Robuchon, and Patricia Wells, first opened my eyes to the diversity of potatoes and endured endless potato debates; Richard Liebowitz of Culinary Specialty Produce, who was extremely generous of his time and his expertise; Richard Blair, who did elegant justice to dozens of stunning and unusual spuds; Jane Dystel, my agent,

who shared my enthusiasm for this subject and made the book possible; and Richard Fabricant, who had no trouble at all enjoying the recipes put before him.

I also owe a debt of thanks to the many Peruvians I chatted with in the markets of Andean villages more than seven years ago, who managed to explain something of their passion for their essential crop and its diversity.

And a hearty thanks to all the growers who donated potatoes for the pictures in the book: Sheldon Rockey of Rockey Farm in Center, Colorado; Rob and Jan Goranson of Goranson Farm in Dresden, Maine; Peter Taines in Penngrove, California; Wally Condon of Small Potatoes in Lodi, California; Jim and Megan Gerritsen of Wood Prairie Farm in Bridgewater, Maine; Al Buehrer and Bill Neely of Indian Rock Produce in Quakertown, Pennsylvania; and, again, Rick Bishop of Mountain Sweet Berry Farm in Roscoe, New York.

Foreword

While potatoes have been around for centuries, these days, most people think of them simply in terms of white or red. But we are increasingly being introduced to an abundance of other varieties. With their assorted creaminess, starchiness, thickness of skin, texture, water content, and color, each kind finds its own niche in the kitchen. Add the fact that potatoes can be fried, baked, roasted, puréed, or boiled to perfection, and they prove to be a most versatile foodstuff.

The true beauty of potatoes is that they perform equally well in supporting roles as they do as the main feature. I generally use potatoes to highlight other foods, and have particular fun pairing such a commonplace ingredient with luxury items such as truffles or caviar. Potatoes and truffles layered in a tartlet and served with a rich meat reduction sauce is an incredibly aromatic, earthy, intensely satisfying dish. On the other hand, roasted fingerling potatoes garnished with crème fraîche and caviar is a light, elegant appetizer that is perfect with a glass of champagne. In any preparation, the most wonderful thing about the potato is its eminent adaptability.

This versatility is highlighted in each of the scintillating recipes in *The Great Potato Book*. Not one to leave any stone, or potato, unturned, Florence takes great advantage of the range of varieties and includes traditional as well as contemporary recipes to delight the reader. I was immediately drawn to the *Crushed Fingerlings with Brown Butter* and the *Roasted Potatoes and Mushrooms in Red Wine Vinaigrette*. The tantalizing recipes for *Creamed Lobster Hash with Caviar* and *Sweet Potato–Squash Pie* offer innovative alternatives to classic dishes. There are recipes in this book to cover any situation, from appetizers and side dishes to entrées.

Whether you serve potatoes as an accompaniment or as a main dish, don't get stuck in a rut. Look around and discover some of the more unusual varieties out there. While the standby Russet is a wonderful potato with its own uses, next time, try the Bintje for fries, the Katahdin in a gratin, or the Carola for a salad. A whole new world of potatoes will open before you.

—CHARLIE TROTTER

THE POTATO AND ITS PAST:

FROM THE HIGH ANDES
TO THE WORLD

"Let them eat potatoes!"

Had Marie Antoinette dismissed the hungry hordes with that palliative in 1789, she might have been more prophetic than condescending, for the potato was poised to sweep France—to create a culinary revolution not unlike the change brought by the tomato in the Italian kitchen. Indeed, the first French cookery book intended for the general population, not just chefs, was called *La cuisine républicaine.* It was written by a Mme Méridiot shortly before the end of the eighteenth century and was devoted *entirely* to potato cookery.

The French have done more than any other culture to exploit the culinary potential of the potato, glorifying it with cream, butter, and even truffles. Chefs and shoppers can routinely buy dozens of different kinds of potatoes in their markets, and every citizen consumes an average of 275 pounds of potatoes each year, more than double what Americans eat, including all our abundant chips and fries.

Although the Gallic love affair with the *pomme de terre* started around the years of the French Revolution, it was a long time coming. It took nearly three hundred years for the potato, which was native to the high Andes in Bolivia and Peru, to be accepted in Europe.

Archaeological evidence suggests that the potato grew wild along the Chilean coast thirteen thousand years ago and was first cultivated more than seven thousand years ago in the Andean plateaus near Lake Titicaca, at altitudes of more than eleven thousand feet. It flourished where corn would not grow.

Early potatoes are thought to have been extremely bitter. Eventually, more than two hundred varieties were cultivated in Peru, scratched into the steeply terraced earth above the clouds. Scientists believe that they were more nutritionally dense than the modern potatoes.

In the Andes, archaeologists have uncovered pottery shaped like potatoes, and Incan units of time were correlated to how long it took potatoes to cook. Even today, the visitor to Peru who travels to Machu Picchu can observe terraced hillsides blanketed with blooming potato plants, their flowers a riot of pinks, blues, whites, and yellows. The peasant farmers still use wooden spades with footrests, called *tacllas*, just as their ancestors did.

The local markets, like the one I visited in Chinchero, are filled with dozens of kinds of white, yellow, red, brown, blue, and purple potatoes, some in tortured shapes, some no bigger than cherries, and some, the *papas lisas*, without skins. All are piled in front of vendors dressed no less colorfully than their produce. In hardscrabble Peruvian villages, this stunning array is not designer food but everyday sustenance.

In some more remote mountain villages, locals continue to freeze-dry their own potatoes, as the Incas did, to make *chuna*. The harvested potatoes are left out to freeze at night and then, as they thaw in the midday sun, they are stomped on or pounded to squeeze out the moisture. This is done repeatedly, over the course of four or five days, resulting in what amounts to freeze-dried potatoes that can be stored for months. Today, *chuna* is also made commercially and is sold throughout the country. Even restaurants in Lima serve it, reconstituted in stews.

Potatoes have the reputation of being bland, but in Peru they're anything but, with variously starchy, waxy, nutty, bitter, or almost sweet flavors, occasionally hinting of cinnamon or anise.

The earliest evidence that Spanish conquistadors in Peru became familiar with the potato dates from around 1530, when a certain Gonzalo Jiménez de Quesada, who was in the first party of conquistadors with Pizarro, came upon them in the Andes. Many priests and soldiers with Pizarro's armies chronicled the conquest, but the definitive description of the potato was reported by Cieza de Leon, who traveled with Pizarro's army in the 1540s, and who finally wrote his account of the conquest in 1553.

The Spaniards were evidently in no hurry to transport potatoes back to the mother country. Most historians speculate that they reached Spain by 1570, and no later than 1573. That's when reference was made to them in documents from the Hospital de la Sangre in Seville. By then, the Spaniards had already become familiar with sweet potatoes from the Caribbean and Central America and had acquired a taste for them. The result is a confusion of names for the potato that persists to this day.

You Say Potato and I Say . . .

Probably no food on earth has given rise to as much confused nomenclature as the potato. I'll try to sort it out.

Potato, in English, is derived from batata, *which is the Caribbean name for sweet potato. It might be derived from* pappus *or* pappa, *an Indian word.* Batata *is the name Hispanics in America use for a kind of sweet potato, the Boniato. Some varieties of the Boniato with deep orange flesh are widely known as yams in the United States. Never mind that the true yam is another tuber, completely unrelated to the potato. It doesn't even resemble one.*

But getting back to the potato . . . batata *and* patata *are also used to connote potato—not sweet potato—in Spain. The Italian term,* patata, *is the same.*

The French sometimes use the term patate *for potato, but most often potatoes are called* pommes de terre, *literally "apples of the earth." Sometimes they're shortened to* pommes, *as in* pommes frites, *or French fries.*

Then there's the situation in Germany, where the potato is a Kartoffel. *If you think that word sounds like truffle, you're correct. Back in the sixteenth century, some of the Spaniards who were pillaging not only the gold and silver in Peru, but also the crops, thought potatoes were a kind of truffle. The idea took hold in Germany (which, in that era, was part of a confederation with Spain, called the Holy Roman Empire, an entity that by that time had nothing to do with Rome).*

Finally, in some regions of France, potatoes are popularly called truffes, or truffles of the poor, so to speak.

The arrival in Europe of the sweet potato, which Columbus found in 1492 on the island of Hispaniola, now Haiti and the Dominican Republic, predated that of the Andean potato, or *Solanum tuberosum,* by nearly a century. Sweet potatoes, it turned out, were easy to grow and very tasty.

But when the Andean potato came on the European scene, first to Spain and then to the rest of Europe, it was greeted most warily. The plant is a member of the deadly nightshade family, in the same botanical group as the tomato, another New World cultivar that took a long time to be accepted.

Evidently, in Spain, potatoes were planted to feed the poor. They became a staple in Galicia, an impoverished northern province. They may also have been shipped to Genoa, Italy, again as food for the lower classes. It's clear that by the end of the sixteenth century they had become familiar fare in Flanders. You can see them in Dutch and Flemish still lifes.

Potatoes gradually made their way to Switzerland and Germany, and to France. In 1600, a Swiss, Olivier de Serres, saw the plant growing in Switzerland, and called it *cartoufle.* By the time of the Thirty Years War, 1618 to 1648, potatoes may have already been planted in eastern France. Evidence exists that by 1621 they were cultivated in Germany.

Everywhere they were introduced, potatoes were destined to feed the poor, a fate that has dogged them to the present in some places, especially Ireland. Until the middle of the eighteenth century and the rise of industrial cities, Europe was regularly beset by famines, as Russia continued to be even in the twentieth century. The threat of famine due to crop failure loomed large, especially in northern Europe. In 1663, the Royal Society in London urged that potatoes be planted as a safeguard against famine. For the same reason, by 1720, Frederick William I of Prussia required that they be grown, a practice that Frederick the Great maintained by royal order in 1750. But when Frederick the Great, one of the earliest promoters of the potato, sent them to Prussia in the 1770s to help relieve the populace's hunger after a serious crop failure, the peasants refused to eat them.

Nowhere, however, was the potato as important a deliverance from famine, and at the same time a cause of it, as in Ireland. Although there is a celebrity theory that Sir Walter Raleigh, who had supposedly been given potatoes by a friend of Sir Francis Drake, planted the tubers in Ireland in the late sixteenth century, and even shared them with his queen, Elizabeth I, most historians believe that potatoes were first planted in County Wicklowe in the 1640s. They saved Ireland from famine in 1728 and 1729, and again in 1740. But the eventual Irish dependence on the potato made it responsible for one of that country's greatest famines, starting in 1845.

It was one of the first clearly documented examples of the risks of monoculture. By then, only one kind of potato was being grown in Ireland, and when the black-spot blight struck, the potatoes were all but wiped out, literally turning putrid as the farmers tried to gather them. The per capita consumption of potatoes at the time was estimated at five and one-half pounds a day, and men even kept their thumbnails long, the better to scrape the skin off a baked or boiled potato. The Irish are still Europe's leading potato-eaters.

By 1911, as a result of the potato famine, with the deaths from starvation and disease and the vast immigration of the Irish to the United States, the population of Ireland had been reduced by half, from 8.5 million before the famine to 4.4 million after. Those who did immigrate to America found themselves in a new home where the potato was flourishing.

The first record of potato cultivation in the American colonies dates from 1719, in Londonderry, New Hampshire, after a roundabout journey over the centuries and finally via Ireland. Potatoes had been brought to Boston by Irish Presbyterian immigrants the year before. Widespread cultivation in New England took hold by the end of the eighteenth century, mainly for cattle fodder and food for slaves. Potato recipes would not be popular in American cookbooks for another forty years.

In the summer of 1772, Thomas Jefferson's careful agricultural diaries noted that he had eaten Irish potatoes from his own garden. Frontier families heading to the West took potatoes with them and planted them. Henry Harmon Spalding, a Presbyterian missionary, tried to teach the Nez Percé Indians how to grow potatoes in Utah in 1836, with the first successful crop harvested in 1838. Brigham Young planted a five-acre potato patch in 1847. The Mormons sold potatoes to the pioneers trekking across the country and to the forty-niners rushing to California to pan for gold. Potatoes were soon growing around the Sacramento area. By midcentury, hundreds of varieties were being cultivated in North America, and the hearty tubers had become a dietary staple.

Some of the Mormons from Utah went north into the Idaho territory. By 1860, potatoes were being sown in Franklin, Idaho, setting the stage for that state's eventual dominance of the American potato scene.

As in Jefferson's day, these potatoes were called Irish potatoes, partly because they were the food of Irish immigrants, but also to distinguish the white-fleshed potato from the sweet potato, which had been grown in the South, and especially in Virginia, since the late sixteenth century, having possibly arrived via Spain and England. (An heirloom sweet potato now being grown in Virginia may be related to those originals.) The ongoing confusion

between white and sweet potatoes even prompted a mistaken theory that the potato originated in Virginia. This misunderstanding was due to John Gerard, an English botanist, who described sweet potatoes as "potatoes of Virginia."

Worldwide cultivation of both these crops was the result of the ease with which they could be transported and planted. Just as the Spaniards brought potatoes from the Americas, and the Irish carried them back to New England, the Portuguese, who became familiar with potatoes in the New World, delivered them to Africa. During the eighteenth century, French missionaries introduced them in China and India.

Unlike grains, which must be threshed, winnowed, ground into meal, and otherwise processed in some fashion before cooking, you can dig up a potato, throw it on the fire or in a pot, and eat it. Let it sprout and you have next season's crop.

Although potatoes were initially relegated to the poor largely because they were considered tasteless, even by the French, it only took a little coaxing and imaginative preparation to change that notion.

We have Antoine-Auguste Parmentier, whose name graces a number of delicious potato dishes, including a potato soup and a beef and potato dish, to thank. Parmentier, an agronomist, came upon the potato while he was in a German prison during the Seven Years War, which began in 1756. He was fed potatoes and survived. After his release, he returned to France convinced of the value of the miraculous tuber and began publishing scientific papers promoting it.

He proved that potatoes could be successfully cultivated, and then presented the king, Louis XVI, with a bouquet of potato flowers. That led to a fad for potatoes, whose blossoms were soon painted on the royal dinner service. Potatoes were even planted as ornamentals in the Tuilleries gardens.

But for dinner? *Non merci.*

Parmentier was too smart to be bested by unreasonable popular prejudice, however, and he resorted to a clever subterfuge to convince the stubborn Parisians to give potatoes a try. As the story goes, in 1785, he planted about an acre of potatoes right in the city, on land given him by the king, and posted guards all around, instructing the sentries to look the other way if the populace attempted to filch his tubers.

That did it. The stage was set for the soaring rise in the potato's popularity in France. By the end of the eighteenth century, Parmentier became known for serving dinners with potatoes in every course, something that chefs today, including Charlie Trotter in Chicago and Daniel Boulud in New York, occasionally attempt.

Unlike the situation in the late eighteenth century in England and Ireland, the French started eating potatoes because they liked them, not because they were trying to forestall starvation. The French also had a fairly sophisticated cuisine going by then, which could not be said for the English or the Irish, even among the aristocracy.

The English were meat-eaters. They disdained vegetables as fit only for the poor. It would take more than a century for the English to want potatoes with their meat or chips with their fish.

In England, in the early nineteenth century, as the Industrial Revolution picked up steam and populations left rural areas for the cities, the workers packed into slums could not rely on their little kitchen gardens.

Getting food to them was a challenge. A sharp decline in home bread baking occurred at the same time. The nutritional slack was picked up by the potato, which, for many, became the safety net to avoid starvation. In 1832, the use of potato flour in bread became legal, and by the middle of the century, baked-potato vendors were hawking their wares in London.

Unlike wheat, potatoes could be grown on small plots near the cities. They could also be stored over the winter and then shipped on barges like coal to market. Potatoes were sustenance for the seamen as well. Lobscouse, a sailor's dinner in the early nineteenth century, was essentially Lancashire hot pot, a stew of meat and potatoes. And although the connection was not made, potatoes, which are rich in vitamin C, also helped prevent scurvy, a vitamin deficiency that had long been a scourge of the Royal Navy.

Like Ireland, Germany, France, Russia, and the United States, England became a potato-loving country. In time, the potato became not only accepted, but even relished around the world. The common potato is the fourth most important vegetable crop after corn, wheat, and rice. Sweet potatoes follow closely, as the world's sixth largest vegetable crop, with 90 percent of them grown in tropical and subtropical regions of Asia. They are an important ingredient in Japanese and Korean cuisines.

Potatoes are now grown and eaten in some one hundred countries. Surprisingly, American potato production accounts for less than 10 percent of the world total. China, where potato dishes are rarely represented in the traditional cuisine, but whose population is often sustained by potatoes, especially in rural areas, has become the number-one producer.

POTATOES TODAY

Decades ago in late summer, after the harvesters had gone through the potato fields near our summer and weekend house in the Hamptons on eastern Long Island, our family and some of our friends would happily glean the tiny potatoes that fell through the fingers of the machines. The farmers had no interest in those under-sized culls, usually an inch or two in diameter, and they would eventually plow them under. But we rescued them to boil up in 10 minutes, douse with sour cream, salt, and pepper, and devour.

Those days are gone. Now baskets of these fresh little beauties share farm-stand space at premium prices, and the forager is out of luck. Potatoes of every size, color, and shape are in demand. Added to the familiar russets or Idahos, California Long Whites, bulky Eastern boiling potatoes, and generic red-skinned "new" potatoes are Yukon Golds, Bintjes, Finnish, and fingerling varieties, to name a few. They range in color from pale ivory to purple and come in assorted shapes, from hefty round to delicately slender.

The potato has a welcome universality unmatched by almost any other food. When someone says "fries" or "mashed" or "chips," the ingredient in question is understood.

It's not surprising, then, that potatoes are the most important fresh produce crop in the world, representing a one-hundred-billion-dollar harvest worldwide. A potato field will yield more calories per acre than one planted with grain, so it made good sense to grow potatoes as a hedge against famine centuries ago, even though the experts at the time were unaware of the nutritional details.

According to the United States Department of Agriculture, in 1999, the major potato-growing states, in order of the size of the harvest, were Idaho, Washington, Wisconsin, Oregon, and North Dakota. New York, once an important grower, is no longer in the top ten, and Maine has slipped to eighth place.

Idaho's dominance is due largely to a discovery, almost by accident, by twenty-three-year-old Luther Burbank. His find was a mutation that became known as the Russet Burbank potato.

In 1872, the young botanist came upon an odd seed ball in his plot of Early Rose potatoes in Lancaster, Massachusetts. He planted the seeds and within two years had a crop of a new type of potato, a large, smooth-skinned oval. He tried to sell the potatoes as a seed crop to several dealers and finally accepted an offer of $150 for some of them, well below the $500 he wanted. He went west to California and planted them there. Shortly there-after, a farmer in Denver began growing the new Burbank potato, but some developed rough brown skins. The Russet Burbank was born.

It took subsequent cultivation in Idaho, which began around 1880, for the potato to flourish, however. Idaho offered perfect growing conditions: light, moist, volcanic soil; sunny days; and cool nights. The potato, originally a high-altitude plant, took well to Idaho's fertile plateaus. And because it turned out to be blight-resistant, the farmers loved it.

Idaho became a state in 1890, by which time potato cultivation had already been established. The Russet Burbank paved the way for the industrialized potato. The factory-made potato chip, based on the Saratoga chip supposedly invented by George Crum at Moon's Lake House in Saratoga Springs, New York, was introduced in 1885. An automatic peeling machine was developed in 1925. Instant mashed potatoes were introduced in 1946. In 1969, the Food and Drug Administration approved the manufacture of potato chips made from dried pota-toes, a.k.a. Pringles.

Annual American potato consumption declined from 200 pounds per person in 1900 to 120 pounds in 1960, but the slippage has now been halted, thanks to frozen French fries and snack foods.

Increasingly, following America's lead, the international crop goes to the processor. More than half of the world's potatoes wind up mechanically chipped, fried, and frozen. In 1983, Simplot, an Idaho company, processed two billion pounds of potatoes. Thirteen years later, their production had doubled. Frozen potatoes have grown into a two-billion-dollar industry.

The industrialization of the potato has resulted in a narrowing of varieties. Although there were forty kinds of potatoes sold worldwide in the late eighteenth century, and an unbelievable one thousand by the early twentieth, only four varieties account for nearly three-fourths of the American production today. One-third of all the potatoes grown in America, and about 99 percent of those grown in Idaho, are Russet or Russet Burbank.

But for those who care, there is a backlash and a growing proliferation of varieties. For example, the French government now recognizes some one hundred varieties as commercially viable, a handful of which have become highly prized by American chefs. As with other categories of produce, chefs, and a growing number of consumers, adore these boutique newcomers, many of them long appreciated in Europe but just beginning to make headway here. The American Russet enjoys an acceptance and versatility that's unmatched in the world, but the new varieties, some of them rediscovered heirlooms once cultivated across the country, are also worth seeking for their often intensely nutty or buttery flavors, unusual shapes, or surprising colors.

Like layers of beaten gold, paper-thin slices of potato might enrobe a fillet of fish. Chefs create signature dishes with voluptuous mashed potatoes. Diced potatoes show up, correctly, in a plate of *linguine al pesto*. On a summer weekend, Zabar's, in New York City, may have fifteen kinds of potato salad on display. Now, from Hawaii to Cape Cod, dozens of high-quality small-batch chip makers are at work, some using purple potatoes and sweet potatoes, and some restaurants are even frying their own chips. Even potato peels have come to be appreciated as a snack food.

Potatoes are often thought of as a staple with a long shelf life, but there is a newfound understanding of truly fresh potatoes, like the ones I gathered years ago in the Hamptons. New potatoes in France are genuinely fresh, harvested in Brittany and in the Loire Valley from May to July. They are as prized as the first bottles of Beaujolais nouveau, and are a harbinger of the main crop, which arrives in the market from August to October.

In Maine, Goranson Farm now takes pride in selling its first-harvest red-skinned potatoes in time for the Fourth of July. "It used to be a tradition in New England to have new potatoes, fresh peas, and salmon for the Fourth," says Jan Goranson, whose father started the farm just after World War II. The "baby reds," as they are called, are so young, fresh, and tender that their skins are almost transparent.

Goranson Farm takes advance orders for these potatoes every spring, and sells every potato it plants. Other small farms, like Wood Prairie Farm, also in Maine; Mountain Sweet Berry Farm in the Catskill Mountains north of New York City; Heirloom Harvest Farm in southern New Jersey; and Bouchey Potatoes near Spokane, Washington, keep increasing the acreage devoted to unusual varieties, both new hybrids and heirlooms. Rockey Farm in Center, Colorado; Ronniger's Organic Farm in Moxie Springs, Idaho; and Small Potatoes in Lodi, California, are specialists in the development and eventual commercialization of these varieties, experimenting with dozens of them all the time.

In the near future, American shoppers can expect to see interesting offerings from these and similar farms, more European varieties, and more of the potatoes that originate in Central and South America, like the skinless *papas lisas* from Peru. Rick Bishop, the owner of Mountain Sweet Berry Farm, is working on a project with Cornell University to establish seed potatoes from traditional Peruvian varieties so they can be grown in the United States.

Several distributors of boutique produce, like Culinary Specialty Produce in New Jersey, Indian Rock Produce in Pennsylvania, and Diamond Organics and Frieda's Finest in California, now have farmers growing specialty potatoes for them under contract. These distributors offer the potatoes to retailers and chefs throughout the country.

At the same time, the agricultural research stations of major universities are working to develop new strains, for both the industrial processors interested in superior chips or fast-food fries and for the fresh market. These researchers are the ones who gave us the now-popular Yukon Gold. All the growing states scramble continuously to keep ahead of pests and blight. At the same time, acreage devoted to organic cultivation is also increasing.

A newfound appreciation for potatoes, their various colors, shapes, and flavors, is taking hold. Potatoes have finally become exceptional as well as everyday.

POTATO PREJUDICES,
THEN AND NOW

Throughout history new foods have not had an easy time of it. The situation has changed somewhat today in America, partly because of widespread travel, which introduces the visitor to unfamiliar foods. But many of the so-called new produce items are not so much new as rediscovered. Think of the more than one hundred kinds of potatoes that were grown on American farms a century ago and how few, in comparison, are sold on the fresh market now.

But it is doubtful that anyone thinks potatoes are poison, as was commonly believed in the seventeenth century. The widespread European prejudice against potatoes was botanical, religious, and social. Looking back, it was also unreasonable, especially since the alternative, in some instances, was starvation.

Botanically, potatoes, along with tomatoes, eggplants, and tobacco, belong to the nightshade family. Nightshades are flowering plants of which at least one, belladonna, is poisonous. Like potatoes, tomatoes were also thought to be toxic, were initially cultivated as a garden ornamental, and had to fight for acceptance at the table.

It is true that badly stored potatoes can develop toxic alkaloids. A greenish tinge is the indicator. Years ago it was a much more serious problem than it is today.

On religious grounds, strict Protestant ministers in Scotland thought potatoes were ungodly because they were not mentioned in the Bible. The faithful in England were also wary of anything that grew so deep in the ground that it could not simply be pulled up like a carrot or a turnip—that it had to be dug. What the devil were those potatoes doing down there?

People were also fearful of a vegetable that made the water in which it was cooked turn dark, believing it would certainly ruin the land for wheat as well.

In early seventeenth-century France, the priests thought potatoes caused leprosy. They were variously reported to have been banned in Besançon and Burgundy for this reason, but the historic record is unclear. Almost as bad as being responsible for a disfiguring and deadly disease, as far as Protestants in some parts of Europe were concerned, was the notion that potatoes were an aphrodisiac and were referred to in that context in Shakespeare's *The Merry Wives of Windsor*.

Even if it turned out that potatoes were safe to eat, they were regarded as socially unacceptable. In America, John Adams once said he would rather suffer and eat potatoes and water than submit to the British crown. In France, the people were so devoted to their bread that they were unwilling to replace it, even when it was extremely poor quality, with potatoes. That bias was overcome by some peasants, however, once they discovered that potatoes would grow in mountainous stretches unsuited for grain. The Dauphiné, in eastern France, was one of the first regions to accept the tuber. *Gratin Dauphinois* (page 59), a glorious potato dish, was the felicitous result. But until well into the nineteenth century, potatoes were lowly fare, considered fit sustenance only for the poor. That belief, along with the fact that potatoes were easy to grow and harvest, convinced many upstanding people that the potato engendered bad habits instead of hard work.

These notions no longer hold sway. But at the same time, the potato continues to suffer from bias. The notion of the poisonous potato is resurfacing, mainly because of the high levels of pesticides and chemicals used in growing them and to prevent sprouting in storage. This is another reason to buy organic potatoes or those grown by small farms. The contemporary dieter readily shuns the potato on the grounds that it is fattening, when the real culprits are the butter, oil, or cream used to prepare it.

Pellegrino Artusi, who wrote the nineteenth-century Italian culinary bible, *The Art of Eating Well*, said, "The potato suffers from the same defect as rice: it is fattening and filling but not nutritious." What goes around comes around.

BUYING AND
STORING POTATOES

It has become easier than ever to buy potatoes. Even supermarkets routinely carry at least six different kinds, a change from the past when you would have been lucky to find three. Produce managers are even paying attention to labeling them properly.

Potatoes are wonderfully forgiving ingredients and, in a pinch, most of the standard supermarket varieties can be used in virtually all the recipes in this book—and in many others—without risking disaster. Consider, for example, how many cookbook recipes call for nothing more specific than "potatoes."

That said, it's important to understand that the characteristics of texture, flavor, moisture, and starch, and often color and shape, can improve a recipe and allow the dish to soar. Potatoes with low moisture and high starch content, for example, are likely to be fluffier and more floury when cooked than a dense yet moist or waxy potato with a smooth or almost creamy texture that holds its shape and doesn't fall apart when sliced. There are actually two kinds of starch in potatoes. A potato referred to as "starchy" with a floury texture is high in amylose starch. The kind of starch in firm, waxy, smooth-textured potatoes is amylopectin, which holds the potato together like pectin in jam.

The freshness of a potato is another factor. Fresh potatoes, recently dug by a local farmer, especially many of the boutique potatoes in this book, are likely to have better flavor and may cook faster than potatoes kept in storage. There are some exceptions, such as the Russet, which has been bred to improve and have more distinctive skins after being stored for a time.

Certain guidelines apply to buying all potatoes, regardless of the type, however. For any given recipe, it's important to select potatoes that are uniform in size, so they'll cook evenly. Potatoes with even contours, without odd bumps, ruts, or twists, will be easier to peel. Look for specimens that show no signs of sprouting, shriveling, or bruising. Sometimes, when potatoes, especially large ones, are harvested or graded, the machinery makes small gouges or cuts in the skin. Avoid any with these scars.

As with most produce, there are government grading standards for potatoes, with U.S. No. 1 designating the largest, most uniform specimens. On a certain level, it's a guarantee of quality. But those cooks who prize tiny potatoes—which would never qualify as U.S. No. 1—just as they might prefer apples that are not huge and unrelentingly shiny red, are better off eyeballing the produce in the market instead of relying on marketing categories.

New crop red- and golden-skinned potatoes should be taut and shiny. The skin of storage potatoes, like Russets, should be of uniform texture, even though some varieties are naturally rough. Patches of soil can easily be washed off.

A green tinge on the skin of a potato, especially a thin-skinned one, indicates poor storage. The green indicates a higher than normal presence of certain potentially toxic alkaloids, namely solanine and chaconine. One small area of green is not harmful and can be pared away, but it's best not to buy potatoes with any sign of greening.

The potato's skin typically reveals a great deal about quality and freshness, but sometimes a potato will have a dark, rotting center, not indicated by the condition of the peel. Discard it or return it to the store.

Extremes of heat and cold do not benefit potatoes. Store them in a dark, airy, cool spot, under a kitchen counter, or in a low cupboard, for example. Keep them in a basket or in an open paper bag, not sealed in plastic, which can act like a greenhouse, causing them to sprout, soften, and rot. Storing potatoes in a bin with onions, as many people do, will quicken the pace of sprouting and spoilage. Raw potatoes should never be refrigerated. The cold will sweeten the flavor and cause the flesh to darken.

Properly stored potatoes will last for up to a week without deteriorating. As potatoes age, their skins thicken, so if you have bought fresh new potatoes, plan to cook them immediately. If potatoes have just started to sprout, the eyes can be trimmed away, but use the potatoes without delay. Discard any that have sprouted heavily or are soft.

Store sweet potatoes like regular potatoes. They do not hold up as long, however. About four days is the maximum shelf life.

PREPARING POTATOES

The first step in preparing potatoes, whether or not they are to be peeled, is to scrub them under running water with a stiff brush.

You can peel a potato with a sharp paring knife, but one of those swivel-bladed peelers will definitely speed up the job and remove less of the flesh. Another approach is to boil or steam potatoes unpeeled, then slip off the skins once they are cooked.

Contrary to popular belief, the skin of the potato is not the most nutritionally dense part. The flesh just beneath the skin is where proportionately more vitamin C, protein, and flavor are concentrated, which is why it's good to remove as little skin as possible when peeling, and why a dish made with unpeeled potatoes, or potatoes peeled after cooking, will be more nutritious than one made with peeled potatoes. Commercial potato producers have big machines that "sand" the skin off the potatoes, removing only what's needed by tumbling them in big, abrasive drums.

Once potatoes have been peeled or cut, an enzyme, polyphenoloxydase, will cause the flesh to darken, much like apples and pears. To prevent discoloration, keep cut potatoes submerged in cold water until ready for use. Sweet potatoes should be handled the same way.

When boiling potatoes, choose a saucepan that will be only about two-thirds full, to avoid boiling over. Start the potatoes in cold water to cover, and once the water comes to a boil, decrease the heat to achieve a steady simmer. Be sure sweet potatoes are submerged at all times, as areas exposed to air can discolor. Unless the recipe specifies parboiling or blanching, the potatoes should be cooked just until the tip of a sharp knife meets no resistance. An average potato, about 2 inches in diameter, will cook in about 20 minutes. (Plan on almost twice this amount of time if steaming.) Drain the potatoes immediately to stop the cooking. A colander works well for this step.

When baking potatoes, rubbing the skin with some olive oil or butter will enhance its crispness. Putting the potatoes directly on the oven rack, without using a pan, will also result in crisper skin. I don't recommend wrapping potatoes in aluminum foil because they tend to get soggy. A microwave may shorten your cooking time, but you probably won't like the results—microwaved potatoes taste more steamed than baked.

For mashing, a ricer that forces the tender potato flesh through screens of tiny holes is best. Plunger-style potato mashers are not as effective in producing a smooth purée. Do not be tempted to use a food processor. It will produce mashed potatoes that have the texture of wallpaper paste. But you can use an electric mixer on slow speed to mash potatoes. Warm the milk or cream you are using for mashed potatoes to keep them fluffy and to minimize the need for lengthy reheating.

Use heavy nonstick skillets for frying potatoes, to achieve even browning. A well-seasoned cast-iron skillet is a good alternative. Butter will enhance browning more than oil. But for the most elegant, golden effect, clarified butter is best. Dry potatoes thoroughly before sautéing or frying them, otherwise the moisture on the surface will inhibit browning and cause spatters.

For deep-frying, I like to use a wok, which requires somewhat less oil than a straight-sided pot or saucepan. Some cookbooks say that the oil from frying potatoes can be recycled, but I always use fresh oil. The best French fries are fried twice, first to seal the surface without browning, then, after the potatoes have been allowed to cool, at higher temperature for a final burnish and crisping.

Another potato specialty, the soufflé potato, is also

fried twice, a technique that was supposedly discovered by accident on August 26, 1837, during the preparation for a banquet for the French king, Louis Philippe. The king was late, so the chefs had to let the fried potatoes cool after they had been cooked. Just before they were finally served, the cooks plunged them into hot oil to reheat them, and they puffed up majestically.

Do not try to freeze cooked potatoes at home, unless they're puréed in a soup. A commercial blast freezer is necessary to prevent cellular changes that will give the potatoes a mealy texture once they thaw. I even remove potatoes from a stew I'm planning to freeze, and cook fresh ones when I reheat the stew. There is no need for long-term storage of leftover potatoes in any case. They are a wonderful resource, for use in salads, soups, croquettes, omelets, and stuffings, to name a few everyday possibilities.

Potatoes can be used in some surprising ways, too. For example, a piece of raw potato cooked in a soup that's too salty will improve the flavor. The water in which potatoes have been boiled makes an excellent soup base. It will also enhance the fermentation when used in bread baking. Mixed with flour and allowed to ferment at room temperature, it becomes a sourdough starter. And you can use the cut side of a half potato to smooth hot caramel on a baking sheet or marble slab.

In large measure potatoes are a blank canvas. In the raw state, their colors and shapes distinguish one variety from the next. But once cooked, it often takes a connoisseur to recognize the subtle differences between them. The flavor of a potato is also usually quite delicate, making it a good foil for other ingredients. That means it is important to select the frequent components of potato recipes with as much care as it is the potatoes themselves.

When potatoes are on the menu, you reach for the salt. Good sea salt or at least kosher salt will provide a truer, cleaner enhancement to a potato's natural flavor than ordinary table salt. In France, many kinds of potatoes are grown near the sea, and the hint of marine taste in the salt from those same areas—from Noirmoutier, an island off the coast of Brittany, for example—makes it a perfect partner for potatoes.

When adding pepper, use it freshly ground. And if little black specks will detract from the dish, substitute freshly ground white pepper.

Butter is frequently paired with potatoes, and it's best to use good-quality unsalted butter. I never use margarine.

Oils for frying should be neutral, with a high smoke point. My preference is for cold-pressed grapeseed oil, but peanut oil and canola oil are also acceptable. Olive oil, always extra virgin, can season potatoes, often in place of butter, be used as a gloss, and can be employed for sautéing, but it is generally not suitable for deep-frying. Italian chefs deep-fry in lesser grades of highly refined olive oil, like virgin or pure. Consider the flavor of the olive oil, and whether the recipe calls for one that is rich and fruity, sharp and peppery, or delicate. Nut oils, especially hazelnut, can add a lovely seasoning touch to potatoes, especially mashed potatoes, and truffle oils, white or black and used sparingly, can be heavenly as well.

Parmesan cheese has to be imported Parmigiano-Reggiano from Italy, freshly grated.

As a rule of thumb, 6 to 8 ounces of potatoes will serve one person.

WHITE POTATOES

The category of white potatoes should probably be renamed brown. It refers to potatoes with snowy flesh but with skin that can range from ivory to deep mahogany. Plenty of potatoes in the red category also have white flesh, but that group goes according to skin color. The white potato category is anchored by the nearly all-purpose Russet.

Creamer

These are endearing potatoes, relatively low in starch and with a velvety texture and a mild, almost mushroomy flavor. As specialty varieties go, Creamers are fairly easy to find. A favorite of Maine farmers, their popularity is now increasing, and they're showing up in other cool regions of the country. Creamers are often harvested golf-ball size but can sometimes be found larger. As their name implies, the flesh takes on a suave creaminess when roasted, sautéed whole, or par-boiled and added to a stew.

SUBSTITUTES: CHARLOTTE, FRENCH FINGERLING, SMALL LONG WHITE

COLD AVOCADO AND POTATO SOUP

YIELD: 6 SERVINGS

Vichyssoise, the famous cold potato and leek soup, was invented in America and not, as one might assume, in France. Louis Diat, a French chef working at New York's Ritz-Carlton hotel before World War I, adapted his mother's recipe for traditional potato and leek soup to create an elegant cold cream soup, which he named vichyssoise after a city near his hometown. There are dozens of variations that call for a base of creamy cold potato purée. In this one, adapted from a recipe in Paris in a Basket, *a wonderful book about Parisian open-air markets by Nicole Aimée Meyer and Amanda Pilar Smith, avocados take the place of leeks, resulting in a velvety summertime pleaser.*

2 ripe Hass avocados, pitted, peeled,
    and coarsely chopped
Juice of 1 lemon
1 1/2 pounds Creamer potatoes, peeled
Salt
4 cups chilled, defatted well-flavored chicken stock
1/2 teaspoon ground cumin
Freshly ground black pepper
Fresh cilantro leaves, for garnish

Mix the avocados with the lemon juice in a bowl. Cover and set aside.

Place the potatoes in a saucepan, cover with cold salted water, bring to a boil, decrease the heat to a simmer, and cook for about 20 minutes, until tender. Drain and chop roughly.

Place half of the potatoes and half of the avocado-lemon mixture in a blender with 1 cup of the chicken stock and the cumin. Process until smooth, gradually adding another cup of the stock. Transfer to a large bowl.

continued

Purée the remaining potatoes and avocados with the remaining 2 cups stock and add to the bowl, mixing well. Season to taste with salt and pepper.

Cover and refrigerate for at least 4 hours, until very cold. Check seasoning and serve chilled, garnished with a few cilantro leaves.

ROASTED POTATOES WITH ROSEMARY

YIELD: 6 SERVINGS

This recipe is high on my potato hit parade. First of all, it couldn't be easier. Second, it's delicious. The only requirement is that the potatoes be uniformly small and that you allow the full hour and a half for roasting. That might seem like a long time for small potatoes, but it's needed for them to acquire a seductively creamy interior to contrast the toasty skin.

2 1/2 pounds small Creamer potatoes, scrubbed and halved
2 tablespoons extra virgin olive oil
Salt and freshly ground black pepper
2 tablespoons fresh rosemary leaves

Preheat the oven to 375°.

Place the potatoes in a baking dish that will hold them in a single layer. Drizzle with the olive oil and sprinkle with salt and pepper to taste and half of the rosemary leaves. Using your hands, toss the potatoes in this mixture until they are well coated.

Place in the oven and bake for 30 minutes. Use a spatula to turn the potatoes and continue baking for 1 hour longer, until very tender and well browned. Scatter the remaining rosemary leaves over them. Check seasoning and serve hot or at room temperature.

Irish Cobbler

A traditional white-flesh potato, medium sized and round, with thin skin, a dense, dry texture, and a nutty flavor, the Cobbler has long been popular in the eastern United States. It has a medium starch content, making it good for mashing, for using in potato cakes, and, of course, for cooking up Irish recipes, most of which can be counted on for some onion or chives to bolster the Cobbler's subtle flavor. For a change of pace, you might try baking the Irish Cobbler, or burying some, wrapped in aluminum foil, in the smoldering coals of a charcoal fire. It's the only way I ever cook foil-wrapped bakers, and they emerge with a delightfully haunting smoky taste.

SUBSTITUTES: KATAHDIN, KENNEBEC, RUSSET

IRISH POTATO-HERB SCONES

YIELD: 8 SERVINGS

Ireland's potato repertory includes an array of dishes designed to recycle yesterday's cooked potatoes. In fact, almost any traditional Irish potato dish, except plain boiled ones or the old-fashioned potatoes roasted over peat charcoal, can be made using leftovers. In this one, which is given in a recipe that starts from scratch but can exploit available leftovers, potatoes are mashed, seasoned with herbs, given some backbone with flour and eggs, cut in triangles, and fried. The results look like scones. They're perfect to serve with a hearty soup—a cabbage soup perhaps.

2 pounds Irish Cobbler potatoes, scrubbed
1 egg, lightly beaten
1 tablespoon minced fresh chives
1 1/2 teaspoons minced fresh parsley
7 tablespoons unsalted butter, at room temperature
1/4 cup all-purpose flour
1/4 cup whole-wheat flour
1 to 2 tablespoons milk, if needed
Salt and freshly ground black pepper

Place the potatoes in a saucepan, cover with cold water, bring to a boil, decrease the heat to a simmer, and cook for about 20 minutes, until tender. Drain and, when cool enough to handle, peel and place in a bowl. Mash them and stir in the egg, herbs, and 3 tablespoons of the butter. Mix the flours together and stir 3 tablespoons of this mixture into the potatoes, reserving the rest. The potatoes should hold their shape but not be too stiff or dry. Add a little milk if necessary to correct the consistency. Season with salt and pepper.

Knead the potato mixture briefly on a work surface and flatten it into a disk about 1 inch thick. Cut the disk into 8 triangles.

Just before serving, spread the remaining flour mixture on a plate and season it with salt and pepper. Dip each potato triangle into the flour mixture to coat lightly. Grease a griddle with some of the remaining butter or melt the butter in a large, heavy skillet, preferably cast iron, over medium heat. Fry the triangles for about 4 minutes on each side, until crusty and browned. Serve at once.

SALMON CAKES WITH GREEN SALSA

YIELD: 8 SERVINGS

Here is a recipe for fish cakes that illustrates the use of leftover mashed potatoes. But these are not ordinary fish cakes, since they call for both fresh and smoked salmon. Leftover salmon is fine. A tangy Southwestern salsa is served alongside.

1 pound fresh salmon, poached
4 ounces smoked salmon, minced
1 cup mashed Irish Cobbler potatoes, cooled
1/4 cup finely chopped scallions
1/3 cup minced fresh cilantro
2 eggs
Salt and freshly ground black pepper
1/2 cup unseasoned dried bread crumbs
2 cups drained canned tomatillos
1 onion, coarsely chopped
1 jalapeño chile, seeded and chopped
2 tablespoons freshly squeezed lime juice
1/4 cup extra virgin olive oil

Flake the poached salmon into a bowl and mix with the smoked salmon, potatoes, scallions, 2 tablespoons of the cilantro, and the eggs. Season with salt and pepper.

continued

Shape into 16 cakes each 3 inches in diameter and ¹/₂ inch thick. Coat evenly with the bread crumbs. Cover and chill for at least 1 hour.

Meanwhile, make the salsa: Combine the remaining cilantro with the tomatillos, onion, chile, and lime juice in a food processor and pulse until finely chopped, not puréed. Transfer to a serving dish and set aside.

Heat the oil in a large nonstick skillet over medium heat. Fry the salmon cakes turning once, for about 8 minutes on each side, until golden brown on both sides and heated through. Serve immediately with the tomatillo salsa.

Katahdin

One of the classic "boiling" potatoes, Katahdins are fairly large, with heavy, deep tan skin; medium starch; and white flesh. They're good all-purpose potatoes grown on Long Island in New York and in Maine. Although excellent in soups, casseroles, gratins, and potato cakes, they are less suited for baking or for salads that call for a waxier potato. However, if you can find tiny, fresh Katahdins, use them in salads, especially with creamy dressings.

SUBSTITUTES: IRISH COBBLER, KENNEBEC

SMASHED POTATOES WITH
RUTABAGA AND GARLIC

YIELD: 4 SERVINGS

Not mashed, smashed. In the old days, these would be called lumpy mashed potatoes, but chefs have dressed up that home-style concept and now offer smashed potatoes. What sets this recipe apart is its blend of potatoes and rutabagas, the latter adding an intriguing flavor dimension to the dish. Roasted garlic delivers extra zestiness. It's a terrific dish to serve with a steak or grilled fish, but not one that takes well to reheating. The garlic can be roasted in advance, but the rest of the dish should be made fresh. Hefty Katahdins are suited to this recipe, though Kennebecs (page 37) and even the ubiquitous Yukon Gold (page 92) can be used.

1 head garlic
4 tablespoons extra virgin olive oil
1 pound Katahdin potatoes, peeled and
    cut into chunks
1 pound rutabagas, peeled and cut into chunks
Salt and freshly ground black pepper

Preheat the oven to 450°. Slice the top ¹/₂ inch off the head of garlic, brush the cut area with about 1 teaspoon of the olive oil, and wrap the head in aluminum foil. Place it in the oven and roast for about 20 minutes, until golden brown.

Meanwhile, place the potatoes and rutabagas in a saucepan, cover with salted water, bring to a boil, decrease to a simmer, and cook for about 20 minutes, until tender. Drain and return the vegetables to the pan.

Squeeze the soft garlic cloves out of the head and add them to the vegetables in the pan along with the remaining olive oil. Roughly smash the ingredients together with

the back of a spoon, a large fork, or a potato masher until
well blended but still lumpy. Season to taste with salt and
pepper. Reheat briefly and serve.

ITALIAN POTATO CAKE

YIELD: 6 SERVINGS

*When Italians mash potatoes, they inevitably use them to
make gnocchi, plump little dumplings. But Bramante, a
small restaurant near the Piazza Navona in Rome, combines mashed potatoes with Parmigiano-Reggiano and
mild mortadella to make a savory potato cake crisped
with bread crumbs. The potato cake, calling for an old-
fashioned masher like Katahdin, can be served as a first
course in its singular glory, as it is at Bramante, or as a
luncheon or supper dish with a salad and another vegetable, wild mushrooms sautéed and moistened with
white wine, for example, or steamed asparagus. It can
also be prepared in advance and reheated.*

2 1/4 pounds Katahdin potatoes, peeled and
    quartered
1 1/2 tablespoons unsalted butter, at room
    temperature
1/4 cup unseasoned dried bread crumbs
3/4 cup freshly grated Parmigiano-Reggiano cheese,
3 ounces mortadella, preferably imported,
    thinly sliced, then minced
2 eggs, lightly beaten
2 to 3 tablespoons milk
Generous pinch of freshly grated nutmeg
Salt and freshly ground black pepper

Place the potatoes in a saucepan with salted water to
cover, bring to a boil, decrease the heat to a simmer, and

continued

cook for about 20 minutes, until tender. Drain and pass through a ricer into a bowl.

Preheat the oven to 400°. Use about 1/2 tablespoon of the butter to grease a 9-inch springform or other loose-bottom baking pan at least 1 1/2 inches deep. Coat the bottom with half of the bread crumbs.

Add the cheese, mortadella, eggs, 2 tablespoons milk, nutmeg, and salt and pepper to taste to the potatoes and mix well. They should be smooth and thick. Add a little more milk if necessary. Spread the potato mixture in the prepared baking pan and smooth the top. Sprinkle with the remaining bread crumbs and dot with bits of the remaining butter.

Bake for about 35 minutes, until the top is golden. Remove from the oven and set aside for about 10 minutes. Remove the sides from the pan and cut the cake into wedges for serving.

Kennebec

The old-fashioned Kennebec, once widely cultivated in Maine, has become something of a rarity. Like the Katahdin, it's a mild-flavored, multipurpose variety used in soups, potato cakes, and frittatas. Stores label these simply "boiling potatoes," and they have a texture that's neither as starchy as the staple Russet nor as waxy as a thin-skinned small red or oval white potato. They're good keepers because they tend to be slow to sprout when stored in a cool, dry place. You'll probably find these medium to large sized.

SUBSTITUTES: IRISH COBBLER, KATAHDIN

POTATO FRITTATA

YIELD: 6 APPETIZER SERVINGS

Potatoes and eggs, both inherently on the bland side, marry well and willingly accept a jolt of forceful seasoning. This frittata, an alluring brunch dish, first course, or, cut into small squares, cocktail nibble, is a good example. Sundried tomatoes, herbs, cheese, and olives provide all the piquancy it needs. The Kennebec is my first choice, but the recipe works extremely well with other East Coast storage varieties like the Katahdin (page 33), too. The frittata is made with twice as many egg whites as whole eggs, to keep the fat content in check.

1 3/4 pounds large Kennebec potatoes, scrubbed and quartered

3 eggs

6 egg whites

Salt and freshly ground black pepper

1/3 cup freshly grated Parmigiano-Reggiano cheese

1 tablespoon slivered fresh basil

2 oil-packed sundried tomatoes, well drained and minced

8 pitted oil-cured black olives, minced

4 tablespoons extra virgin olive oil

Place the potatoes in a saucepan with water to cover, bring to a boil, decrease the heat to a simmer, and cook about 25 minutes, until tender. Drain, allow to cool briefly, then peel and slice.

Beat the eggs and egg whites together with salt and pepper. Stir in the cheese, basil, sundried tomatoes, and olives.

Heat half of the olive oil in a 12-inch nonstick or well-seasoned cast-iron skillet over medium-high heat. Spread the potato slices in the oil and cook for about 5 minutes, until they begin to brown, then turn them to brown the second side lightly. Season with salt and pepper.

Add the remaining oil to the pan. Pour in the egg mixture and cook over medium heat for about 3 minutes, until the eggs are lightly browned on the bottom. Loosen them around the edges with a spatula and shake the pan to make sure the frittata is loose in the pan. Place a large plate upside down over the pan, invert the frittata onto the plate, then slide it back into the pan to brown the other side for 2 to 3 minutes. Transfer to a serving platter and cut into wedges to serve.

Alternatively, after inverting the frittata in the pan, the skillet can be placed under a hot broiler for 1 to 2 minutes to cook the top, then be served directly from the skillet.

Long White

Also called White Rose and California Long White, this is a medium-large, white-fleshed potato with thin speckled beige skin, a nutty flavor, and moderate starch content. Until recently it was the best substitute for many European potatoes like the Ratte and the Bintje. Small ones tend to be rounder than the larger ones, which are elongated. Long Whites are widely available and are very good to sauté, their moderate starch content making them less likely to stick in the pan. Medium-sized ones are splendid peeled, rolled in butter in a heavy skillet, then covered and cooked until tender. Just shake the pan from time to time so they are burnished on all sides. They can be used for braising and in salads, too.

SUBSTITUTES: BINTJE, CREAMER, MARIS PIPER

POTATOES STEAMED WITH BACON

The advantage to steaming potatoes instead of boiling them is that they emerge tender but dry. For this recipe, in which the potatoes become coated with bacon and drippings, the dry texture balances the fat. The round, small Long White is excellent here, although the Creamer (page 26) or Red Bliss (page 107) would be nearly as good. Be sure to use good-quality smoked country bacon, not the everyday supermarket stuff.

2 pounds small Long White potatoes, peeled
1/4 pound slab bacon, in thick slices
2 tablespoons minced shallots
2 tablespoons cider vinegar
Salt and freshly ground black pepper
1 teaspoon fresh thyme leaves

Steam the potatoes for about 30 minutes, until tender. While the potatoes are steaming, fry the bacon in a large skillet over medium heat until it is lightly browned. Remove the bacon from the pan, reserving the fat in the pan, and drain on paper towels until cool. Chop the bacon.

Add the shallots to the bacon fat in the skillet and sauté over medium heat for about 2 minutes, until they just begin to brown. Remove the pan from the heat and stir in the vinegar.

When the potatoes are tender, transfer them to a serving dish. Fold in the bacon fat mixture and season to taste with salt and pepper. Scatter the bacon and thyme leaves on top, then serve.

POTATO AND KALE SOUP
WITH SCALLOPS

YIELD: 8 SERVINGS

Fresh sea scallops mated with potatoes and sharpened with sausage and kale make a lusty, chowderlike soup, a lovely starter for a cold-weather dinner. Almost any moderately starchy white potato will suit this dish. Long Whites are easy to come by.

1/3 cup extra virgin olive oil

3/4 pound sea scallops, halved horizontally

6 ounces kielbasa or other garlic sausage, coarsely diced

1 large onion, chopped

4 cloves garlic, smashed

1 1/2 pounds medium Long White potatoes, peeled and sliced 1/2 inch thick

8 cups water

Salt and freshly ground black pepper

5 cups packed finely shredded green kale, without stems

Crushed red pepper flakes

Heat 2 tablespoons of the oil in a heavy skillet, preferably nonstick, over high heat. Add the scallop pieces and sear quickly for about 1 minute on each side. Remove them and set aside.

Add the sausage to the skillet and cook over medium heat for 6 to 8 minutes, until lightly browned. Add 1 tablespoon of the oil to the pan and sauté the onion and garlic for 3 to 4 minutes, until tender but not brown. Transfer these ingredients to a large, deep saucepan. Add the potatoes and water and bring to a boil. Season to taste with salt and pepper and simmer for about 15 minutes, until the potatoes are tender. Briefly mash the potatoes in the pot, leaving plenty of pieces.

Add the kale and simmer for 5 to 10 minutes, until wilted. Add the scallops and the remaining olive oil. Bring to a simmer and adjust the seasonings, adding red pepper flakes to taste. Serve hot.

SHALLOT POTATOES

Potatoes marry especially well with members of the onion family. Leeks, garlic, onions, chives, scallions, and shallots are all superb complements for a host of potato dishes. In this simple example, the potatoes are gently simmered with shallots and just enough stock, so that by the time the potatoes are tender they have also absorbed the liquid and become infused with its flavor and the provocative mellowness of the shallots. The recipe requires potatoes that will hold their shape and not become mushy. Smooth, easily peeled Long Whites are my choice.

3 tablespoons unsalted butter

1 cup diced shallots

6 cups peeled and diced Long White potatoes
     (about 4 large potatoes)

1 1/2 cups well-flavored chicken stock

Salt and freshly ground black pepper

3 tablespoons minced fresh flat-leaf parsley

Melt the butter in a heavy 3-quart saucepan over medium heat. Add the shallots and sauté, stirring, for about 4 minutes, until soft but not brown. Stir in the potatoes and continue cooking several minutes longer, until the potatoes are coated with butter. Add the stock, bring to a simmer, and season to taste with salt and pepper.

Reduce the heat to low, cover tightly, and cook for about 20 minutes. The potatoes should be tender and have absorbed most of the stock. Fold in the parsley and serve.

Maris Piper

The Maris Piper is a white-fleshed, starchy potato that's a close cousin to the Bintje (page 64), though perhaps a trifle less refined. Like the Bintje, it comes from Belgium, where it is quite popular. Farmers in the United States have started to discover its considerable attributes. The best uses are frying and in gratins.

SUBSTITUTES: BINTJE, LONG WHITE, RUSSET

CURRIED CUCUMBER-POTATO SOUP

YIELD: 6 SERVINGS

A potato that will provide smooth texture and body is what's needed for this soup, which combines cucumbers and apples with the potatoes. The moderate starch content is enough to keep the yogurt from separating if the soup is served hot, instead of the more typical cold. White Maris Pipers, Bintjes (page 64), or Long Whites (page 40) are best, although Yukon Golds (page 92) will also complement the curry.

2 tablespoons extra virgin olive oil

1 large onion, finely chopped

2 cloves garlic, minced

$1/2$ Granny Smith apple, peeled, cored, and chopped

$1 1/2$ teaspoons ground cumin

2 teaspoons curry powder

$1/2$ pound Maris Piper potatoes, peeled and diced

2 cups water

2 cucumbers, peeled, seeded, and diced

$1 1/2$ cups plain yogurt

Salt and freshly ground black pepper

1 tablespoon finely chopped fresh mint

Heat the olive oil in a heavy saucepan over low heat. Add the onion and sauté for about 3 minutes, until it begins to soften. Add the garlic, apple, cumin, and curry powder and cook, stirring, for 2 to 3 minutes. Add the potatoes and water, cover, and cook for about 20 minutes, until the potatoes are tender.

Add the cucumbers, remove the pan from the heat, and allow the soup to cool briefly, then purée in a blender or food processor.

If serving cold, refrigerate the soup for at least 4 hours. Stir the yogurt into the soup, season to taste with salt and pepper, and serve with a scattering of mint.

If serving hot, do not refrigerate the soup. Reheat it to a simmer, whisk in the yogurt, season to taste with salt and pepper, and sprinkle with mint before serving.

Russet

The quintessential American potato, the Russet is sold everywhere. It's typically a large, elongated oval with white flesh, a high starch content, and a lightly nutty flavor. It's the potato that's best known as the Idaho, thanks to the happy marriage of the proper soil, climate, humidity, and elevation that allows the Russet, and especially the Russet Burbank, to flourish and reach peak flavor. Depending on the particular variety, the skin can vary from medium tan with some dappled spots, or russeting, to very dark brown. (In agriculture, the term *russeting* is often applied to fruit, like pears and grapefruit, to indicate a pattern of tiny brown spots on the skin. In these fruits it is a sign of sweetness.)

Russet Burbank (developed by Luther Burbank), Norgold Russet, Goldrush, and Russet Norkotah are a few of the varieties developed mainly by university agriculture specialists and grown not only in Idaho but elsewhere in the country. Russets account for almost all of Idaho's crop and about one-third of all the potatoes grown in the United States. The different kinds of Russets have been the result of cross-breeding, to improve the quality of the potato in the field, in the processing plant, and sometimes, on the plate. But the Russet Burbank is generally recognized as one of the best. Unfortunately, it's the rare market that labels these potatoes according to the particular strain. Although the Russet is not especially suited for salad making or for use in recipes that call for tender, young potatoes, it works fine in most other dishes. But it's best as a baker.

SUBSTITUTES: NONE

BASIC BAKED POTATOES

YIELD: I SERVING

Baking—or roasting—a whole potato until it's tender and can be scooped out of its shell must be among the oldest cooking methods in the potato repertory. Today, large oval russets, variously Russet Burbanks, Norgold Russets, or, popularly, Idahos, are the potatoes of choice for baking because of their unifom size and shape and their dry-textured, fluffy flesh. Rubbing the skin with some olive oil or butter before the potatoes go in the oven is an optional step designed to enhance the crispness of the potato shell. It also seals the skin, slightly reducing the baking time. But wrapping them in foil is not recommended, as it tends to make the potatoes soggy. I like putting the potatoes directly on the oven rack, which produces a crispier skin. When I use an electric oven instead of a gas oven, I turn the potatoes once or twice during baking because the heating element is exposed, not insulated from the oven floor as in a gas oven. The microwave can shave many minutes from the preparation time, but the results are uneven and not always the most palatable, tasting more steamed than baked. A better way to speed up the baking in the oven is to insert a metal skewer the length of the potato.

1 Russet potato
1 teaspoon butter or vegetable oil
Butter or olive oil for serving
Salt and freshly ground black pepper

Preheat the oven to 450°.

Scrub the potato and dry well. If desired, rub the skin with the butter. Prick the skin in 1 or 2 places with a skewer or the tines of a fork. Place the potato in the oven and bake for 45 minutes to 1 hour, until the potato offers no resistance when a knife tip is inserted.

Remove the potato from the oven and serve at once whole, or score the potato with an *X*, squeeze the sides to force the *X* open, and then serve with plenty of butter, seasoned to taste with salt and pepper.

Baked Potato Variations

BAKED POTATOES ON THE GRILL

YIELD: 6 SERVINGS

These potatoes carry a smoky flavor, perfumed with fresh rosemary, that makes them delicious accompaniments to grilled meats. They taste best if they are just baked, not leftover and coming from the refrigerator.

6 medium Russet potatoes, freshly baked
4 tablespoons extra virgin olive oil
Salt and freshly ground black pepper
12 small rosemary sprigs

Prepare a fire in a charcoal grill or preheat a gas or electric grill.

Cut the potatoes in half lengthwise. Brush the cut side of each half with some of the olive oil, season to taste with salt and pepper, and embed a rosemary sprig into the surface of each.

Place the potatoes cut side down on the grill. Grill the potatoes for about 10 minutes, until heated through and brown grill marks appear on the surface. Watch carefully and do not allow the potatoes to blacken. Serve hot.

STUFFED BAKED POTATOES

YIELD: 8 SERVINGS

The way to turn a simple baked potato into party fare is to scoop out the filling, mash it with butter and cream, pack it back into the shell, and bake it until the top is crusty. It's also an excellent way to prepare baked potatoes in advance. The stuffed potatoes can idle, on hold, for several hours and be returned to the oven for baking just before serving. The onion addition is not essential, but it does lift the recipe out of the ordinary. As to whether to use plain milk or something richer, like half-and-half, heavy cream, or sour cream, that's up to you. You can also dress this recipe up by adding any one or more of a number of different ingredients to the potato stuffing: minced fresh herbs, grated cheese, crumbled crisp bacon, a little chopped cooked spinach or mushrooms, or even some diced cooked lobster. Or keep it simple, with just some minced chives perhaps, and then add a classy topping of sour cream and good caviar after baking.

4 large Russet potatoes

3 tablespoons unsalted butter or olive oil

1 large onion, finely chopped

1/4 cup milk, half-and-half, heavy cream,
    plain yogurt, or sour cream

Salt and freshly ground black pepper

Preheat the oven to 450°.

Scrub the potatoes and dry well. Prick the skin of each in 1 or 2 places with a skewer or the tines of a fork. Place the potatoes in the oven and bake for about 1 hour, until tender.

While the potatoes are baking, heat 1 tablespoon of the butter in a skillet over medium heat. Add the onion and sauté for about 6 minutes, until golden brown. Set aside.

When the potatoes are done, cut each in half lengthwise. Scoop out all the insides into a bowl, taking care not to break the skins. Use a fork to mash the potato with the remaining butter. Mix in the milk and season with salt and pepper. Fold in the sautéed onion.

Spoon the filling back into the potato skins, making 8 stuffed halves. Lightly trace a crosshatch pattern on top of each with the tines of a fork. (The stuffed potatoes can be set aside for up to 2 hours before baking.)

Place the potatoes on a baking sheet and return to a 450° oven for 15 to 20 minutes, until the potatoes are heated through and lightly browned on top. Serve at once.

SAGE POTATO CHIPS

I have Venetian-born Francesco Antonucci, chef and co-owner of Manhattan's Remi restaurant, to thank for this magical recipe. Fresh sage leaves are sandwiched between thin slices of potato, glued together, so to speak, by the potato starch. They're buttered and baked, emerging crisp and brown with a shadow of the herb. A dusting of salt is all that's needed before these elegant "chips" are ready to serve. And they're guaranteed to disappear before you know it. The only potato that works for this recipe is the Russet. Select well-shaped oval ones.

1/2 cup clarified unsalted butter
3 large Russet potatoes, peeled
36 fresh sage leaves
Fine sea salt or kosher salt

Preheat the oven to 350°. Line 2 large baking sheets with parchment paper and brush the paper with some of the butter.

Using a mandoline or an electric slicer, very thinly slice the potatoes lengthwise. Keep the slices in order, as if you were going to reconstruct the potatoes. You should have 72 slices in all.

Take the slices 2 at a time and sandwich 1 sage leaf between each pair. As the pairs are assembled with the sage, place them on the baking sheet and brush them lightly with the butter.

Place in the oven and bake for 15 to 20 minutes, turning them once as the edges brown. Remove the baking sheets from the oven and transfer the potato "sandwiches" to racks to cool. Dust lightly with salt and serve.

MY MOTHER'S POTATO NOODLES

YIELD: 4 SERVINGS

High-starch, floury potatoes provide the best raw material for all sorts of delicate dumplings and pasta. My mother often made what she called potato noodles, enlisting me to help roll and cut them. She served them tossed with buttered bread crumbs and onions. In her day, with many fewer choices in potato varieties available, she relied on russets.

1 large Russet potato, peeled and cut into chunks

1 egg, lightly beaten

Salt

2/3 to 3/4 cup all-purpose flour

3 tablespoons unsalted butter

1 large onion, sliced

1/4 cup unseasoned dried bread crumbs

Place the potato in a saucepan, cover with water, bring to a boil, decrease the heat to simmer, and cook for about 20 minutes, until tender. Drain, pass through a ricer into a bowl, and allow to cool to room temperature. Stir in the egg and season with salt. Add enough flour to make a soft but manageable dough.

Transfer the dough to a floured board and knead lightly for 1 to 2 minutes, until easy to handle. Roll or pat the dough into a rectangle about 8 by 12 inches and 1/4 inch thick. Cut into strips 1/4 inch wide, and cut the strips into 1-inch lengths.

Melt the butter in a large skillet over medium heat. Add the onion and sauté, stirring frequently, for 8 to 10 minutes, until tender and golden. Stir in the bread crumbs. Remove from the heat.

Bring a large pot of salted water to a boil. Drop in the noodles, decrease the heat to medium, and simmer for about 3 minutes, until they rise to the surface. Drain the noodles in a colander. Briefly reheat the onion mixture, add the noodles to the skillet, and toss gently to coat. Season to taste with additional salt, if necessary, then serve.

WATERCRESS, POTATO, AND SCALLION SOUP

YIELD: 3 OR 4 SERVINGS

The French classic, a purée of leeks and potatoes, lends itself to almost infinite variations. In this one, scallions take the place of the leeks, and watercress adds a refreshing, peppery note and verdant color. The soup can be served hot or cold. But if you're planning to serve it cold, it's best to purée it in a blender, which will yield smoother results than a food processor. To serve hot, it matters less. The reliable Russet potato works best and illustrates yet another use for this versatile staple.

1 tablespoon extra virgin olive oil

5 scallions, finely chopped

1 large Russet potato, peeled and coarsely chopped

3 cups chicken stock, vegetable stock, or water

1 bunch watercress, rinsed and coarsely chopped

2/3 to 3/4 cup low-fat milk

Salt and freshly ground black pepper

1/4 cup heavy cream, or more to taste

Heat the olive oil in a 3-quart saucepan over low heat. Add 4 of the scallions and sauté for about 1 minute, until they turn bright green. Add the potato and stock, raise the heat to medium-high, bring to a boil, decrease the heat to a simmer, and cook for about 25 minutes, until the potato is very tender. Stir in the watercress and remove from the heat. Allow to cool for at least 10 minutes.

Purée the contents of the saucepan in a blender or food processor. Add the milk, purée again, and season to taste with salt and pepper. Return the soup to the saucepan and stir in the cream. Reheat and serve, sprinkled with the remaining scallion. Alternatively, the soup can be chilled for at least 4 hours and served cold.

POTATO AND ONION
FOCACCIA

YIELD: 4 SERVINGS

Focaccia, a thick, yeasted flatbread, takes to many top-pings, much like a pizza. It's especially good paved with potato slices. The nutty, slightly earthy flavor a good Russet acquires when it's baked in the oven also emerges on this focaccia. The bread is best served warm.

1 package active dry yeast

Pinch of sugar

1 cup warm water

4 tablespoons plus 1¹/2 teaspoons extra
    virgin olive oil

Coarse salt and freshly ground black pepper

About 3 cups all-purpose flour

1 onion, sliced paper-thin

Cornmeal, for dusting

1 large Russet potato, peeled

Leaves from 3 rosemary sprigs, or 1 teaspoon dried

Mix the yeast with the sugar in a large bowl. Add 1/4 cup of the warm water and set aside for about 5 minutes, until the mixture becomes foamy. Stir in the remaining 3/4 cup water, 2 tablespoons of the olive oil, 1/2 teaspoon salt, and a generous grinding of fresh pepper.

Stir in 2 to 2 1/2 cups of the flour, 1/2 cup at a time, until a dough forms. Sprinkle with some of the remaining flour and knead in the bowl for about 5 minutes, adding more flour as necessary to keep the dough from becoming too sticky. Brush the dough with a little of the oil, turn it in the bowl, and brush the underside. Cover with a cloth and set aside to rise until doubled, about 1 hour.

While the dough is rising, heat 1 tablespoon of the olive oil in a skillet over medium heat. Separate the onion into rings and sauté for 2 to 3 minutes, until soft but not brown. Set aside. *continued*

Preheat the oven to 500°. Lightly oil a 12- or 14-inch pizza pan and dust it with cornmeal.

Punch the dough down and roll or stretch it to a 12-inch circle. Place it on the pan, prick it all over at 1-inch intervals with a fork, and brush it with 1 tablespoon of the olive oil. Cut the potato in half lengthwise, then slice the halves paper-thin. Arrange the half-moon slices, slightly overlapping, over the dough. Scatter the onion over the top and sprinkle with the rosemary and remaining olive oil. Dust with salt and pepper.

Bake for about 15 minutes, until the dough is brown and the onion and potato slices are also beginning to brown around the edges. Cut into quarters and serve.

GRATIN DAUPHINOIS

YIELD: 6 SERVINGS

Among the simplest ways to glorify potatoes is to bake them in cream with garlic, a sinfully rich classic that originated in a mountainous region in eastern France. A potato with a high starch content, like the Russet, helps thicken the cream, and with russets you can also spare much of the fat by using milk instead. The gratin can be held, once it has finished baking, loosely covered in a warm oven for up to 30 minutes.

1 tablespoon unsalted butter

3 cups half-and-half

4 cloves garlic, smashed

3 pounds Russet potatoes, peeled and sliced
     $^{1}/_{8}$ inch thick

Salt and freshly ground white pepper

Preheat the oven to 350°. Butter a 6-cup gratin dish or baking dish 1$^{1}/_{2}$ to 2 inches deep.

Place the half-and-half in a 3-quart saucepan. Add the garlic and potatoes and bring to a simmer. Season with salt and pepper. Simmer for 5 minutes, then transfer to the prepared gratin dish.

Place in the oven and bake for about 40 minutes, until the top is golden brown, the potatoes are tender, and much of the half-and-half has been absorbed. Serve hot.

GRATIN SAVOYARD VARIATION: Substitute well-flavored beef or chicken stock for the cream and you have a lighter dish, a gratin Savoyard. It's especially good with a topping of shredded Gruyère cheese dotted with butter. Sautéed mushrooms can also be added to it, and crumbly goat cheese can be substituted for the Gruyère.

GOLD POTATOES

This newly fashionable category is the easiest to define. It includes potatoes with yellow flesh, from deep ivory to gold. Usually the skins are golden, too. The now-ubiquitous Yukon Gold, or generic gold potatoes, not specifically Yukons, can be used in place of just about any of the more unusual flaxen potatoes.

Austrian Crescent

These moderately waxy, medium-sized potatoes, with their golden flesh beneath straw-colored skin, beckon from baskets in farmers' markets around New York where they're mostly grown by farmers in the Hudson Valley. The skin is fairly thin—indeed, it almost disappears when the gracefully elongated, nutty-flavored potato is boiled and rolled in butter. We have chefs to thank for the increased availability of fingerlings. Chefs love the way they look on the plate.

SUBSTITUTES: RATTE, RUSSIAN BANANA, RUBY CRESCENT

CRUSHED FINGERLINGS WITH BROWN BUTTER

YIELD: 2 SERVINGS

Michelin three-star chef Joël Robuchon is famous for his satiny potato purée, which calls for nearly as much butter, by weight, as potatoes. He also likes to crush steamed Ratte potatoes ever so lightly, then crisp them in brown butter. Here's an adaptation that's excellent made with lovely fingerlings like Austrian Crescents or golden Russian Bananas (page 87). It's an inventive way to prepare a small potato—halfway between mashed and fried.

3/4 pound Austrian Crescent potatoes, scrubbed

3 cloves garlic, peeled but left whole

3 sprigs thyme

3 tablespoons unsalted butter

Salt and freshly ground black pepper

Place the potatoes in a single layer in a steamer basket. Put the garlic and thyme in the water under the basket, bring to a boil, cover, and steam the potatoes for about 40 minutes, until tender.

Place the potatoes in a single layer in a plastic food-storage bag on a work surface. With the palm of your hand, gently flatten the potatoes to about 1/2 inch thick. Remove the potatoes from the bag and strip off the peels, if desired.

Just before serving, melt the butter in a large, heavy skillet over medium-high heat. Continue heating until the butter turns amber. Place the crushed potatoes in the skillet and sauté, turning once, for about 5 minutes total, until golden brown on both sides. Remove from the skillet, season with salt and pepper, and serve at once.

Bintje

A European favorite, especially for French fries, cultivation of this variety has only recently started in the United States, mostly by small farmers in the East—and it's about time. American cooks have been deprived of this fine potato, which is everyday fare in Europe, for too long. It's of Dutch origin but also widely cultivated in Belgium, the country that insists *it* invented *frites*. The Bintjes that are currently available in American farmers' markets are on the small side, while in Europe they can be quite large, making them easy to peel and cut into uniformly neat ¼-inch-thick sticks for French fries. American Bintjes are delicious to sauté whole in butter, then stew with parsley, or to use for hash browns. The Bintje is a medium-starch potato with pale yellow flesh and a slightly earthy flavor. The peel is not too heavy.

SUBSTITUTES: MARIS PIPER, LONG WHITE, RUSSET

PERFECT FRENCH FRIES

Among the simplest, most ubiquitous, and tempting potato preparations are frites, *or French fries. Of course, a number of megacorporations in the food-service business have perfected the technique of freezing potato sticks for quick reheating or frying, but these industrialized versions cannot compare with the real thing. A mound of perfect* frites *depends on several elements. First, you need a starchy potato, so that moisture does not dilute the oil. Commonplace Russets (page 48) are good, and their size makes them easy to cut properly, but Bintjes and Maris Pipers (page 45) are the choice of Belgian French-fry masters. A wok or deep sauté pan in which about 8 cups of oil, or a depth of about 3 inches, can be heated is crucial. Finally, the technique of partially frying the potatoes, and then frying them again later is what makes all the difference, as it crisply seals the outside and gives a creamy texture within. Eat up: Good French fries wait for no one.*

3 pounds Bintje potatoes, the larger the better
Grapeseed, peanut, or canola oil, for deep-frying
Sea salt or kosher salt

Peel the potatoes and cut lengthwise into 1/4-inch-thick sticks with a knife, a French-fry cutter, a mandoline, or a food processor. Place them in a bowl of cold water to cover.

Heat the oil to a depth of 3 inches in a deep sauté pan, a wok, or an electric deep-fryer to about 300°. Line a large colander with several layers of paper towel.

Drain the potatoes and pat them dry on paper towels. Plunge one-fourth of the potatoes into the oil and cook for 5 to 6 minutes, stirring them around once or twice, until they turn pale gold but have not begun to brown.

continued

When they are done, use a large skimmer to transfer them to the colander. Repeat with the remaining potatoes. Set the parcooked potatoes aside for at least 20 minutes or up to 3 hours.

Just before serving, reheat the oil to 375°. Remove the potatoes from the colander and reline the colander with fresh paper towels. When the oil is hot, cook the potatoes, in several batches, for about 2 minutes per batch, until they are golden brown. Transfer them to the colander when they are done.

When all the potatoes have been cooked, gently toss them in the colander, pull out the paper towels, dust them with salt, and gently toss again. Serve at once.

Carola

Suddenly a darling of the market farmer, the Carola is one of the potatoes that connoisseurs, especially chefs, seek out. You won't find it in a supermarket—not yet at any rate—so do your shopping for the Carola in farmers' markets or by mail order on the Internet. It's a medium-sized, rounded oval, harvested young, with thin, shiny straw-beige skin and a toasty, slightly sweet flavor. A relatively low starch content makes it a fine choice for roasting and even for salads.

SUBSTITUTES: CHARLOTTE, RATTE, YUKON GOLD

PIZZOCCHERI CASSEROLE

Not many pasta recipes are made with potatoes. One classic is linguine al pesto. *As it's made in Liguria, both diced potato and pieces of green bean are often folded into the dish. Another pasta and potato combination is* pizzoccheri, *a hearty winter casserole from the Valtellina, a mountainous region in northern Lombardy. For this dish, sturdy buckwheat noodles are baked with potatoes, cabbage, and cheese. A golden potato is an excellent candidate. Carolas, if they're available, are my choice. Otherwise, Yukon Golds (page 92) are fine. The buckwheat noodles might be even more difficult to secure than the Carola potatoes. Spinach or mushroom fettuccine can be substituted.*

4 tablespoons unsalted butter

1 cup thinly sliced onion

2 large cloves garlic, chopped

1 tablespoon chopped fresh sage

1/2 pound Carola potatoes, peeled and thinly sliced

2 cups shredded savoy cabbage

1 pound *pizzoccheri* (Italian buckwheat *tagliatelle*)
    or spinach fettuccine

Salt and freshly ground black pepper

6 ounces Italian fontina, Taleggio, or *montasio*
    cheese, thinly sliced

1/3 cup freshly grated Parmigiano-Reggiano cheese

Heat 1 tablespoon of the butter in a large skillet over medium heat. Add the onion and sauté for 5 to 6 minutes, until golden brown and starting to crisp. Add the garlic, sauté briefly, then stir in the sage. Remove from the heat and set aside.

Preheat the oven to 400°. Use about ¹/₂ tablespoon of the butter to butter a 9 by 13-inch baking dish.

Bring a large pot of salted water to a boil. Add the potatoes and cook for about 5 minutes, until not quite tender. Add the cabbage and continue cooking for 5 minutes longer. Add the noodles, stir, and cook for another 5 minutes, then drain the contents of the pot, reserving about ¹/₂ cup of the cooking water.

In a large bowl, gently toss the potatoes, cabbage, and noodles with the remaining 2 ¹/₂ tablespoons butter. Season the mixture to taste with salt and pepper. Add the sliced cheese and toss gently again. The cheese will start to melt. Add as much of the reserved cooking water as needed to create a mixture that is moist but not soupy. Spread the mixture in the prepared baking dish.

Sprinkle the onion and garlic mixture and the Parmigiano-Reggiano cheese over the top. Bake for 12 to 15 minutes, until heated through and the cheese on top has melted. Serve at once.

Charlotte

Here's a French potato that has caught the fancy of American farmers, especially those that cater to the needs of top chefs. And with good reason. It's a charming small oval, with pale gold flesh, thin straw-colored skin, and a distinctive note of sweetness in its flavor. Charlottes are harvested when they're young and are best used in recipes that call for steamed, boiled, or sautéed lightly seasoned potatoes, allowing the medium-starch but flavorful Charlottes to shine.

SUBSTITUTES: CAROLA, RATTE, YUKON GOLD

BRAISED POTATOES WITH TURNIPS AND CARROTS

YIELD: 4 TO 6 SERVINGS

Because most root vegetables of similar size cook at about the same rate, it's easy to combine them, as in this tender mixture of potatoes, turnips, and carrots braised in chicken stock with a hint of ginger. Small red potatoes or golden-fleshed potatoes, notably Charlottes, are my choice for this dish. The fallback would be Yukon Golds (page 92). As with the potatoes, try to select turnips and carrots that are uniform in size.

1 pound small white turnips, peeled

1/2 pound carrots, peeled

4 tablespoons unsalted butter

1 1/2 teaspoons peeled and finely slivered
    fresh ginger

1 pound small Charlotte potatoes, peeled

Pinch of freshly grated nutmeg

1 cup well-flavored chicken stock

Salt and freshly ground black pepper

Halve or quarter the turnips, so they're about the same size as the potatoes. Slant-cut the carrots in slices 1 inch long.

Select a heavy saucepan or skillet large enough to hold the vegetables in no more than 2 layers. Melt the butter in the pan over medium heat. Add the ginger and sauté for about 5 minutes, until it softens. Add the potatoes and sauté over medium-high heat for 5 minutes, tossing frequently so they become coated with butter and golden.

Stir in the turnips and carrots. Add the nutmeg and stock and season with salt and pepper. Cover, decrease the heat to very low, and cook, shaking the pan from time to time, for about 25 minutes, until the vegetables are tender. Serve at once or set aside for up to 2 hours and reheat briefly just before serving.

PARSLEY POTATOES

The classic parsley potato, once a commonplace accompaniment for fish, has faded from view. Perhaps it's not sufficiently complex or out-of-the-ordinary for modern tastes. Nonetheless, the recipe belongs in the culinary repertory. Proper cooking of small to medium, uniform-sized potatoes is strictly a matter of time and testing. But the potato of choice should be a full-flavored one because, except for the butter, salt, and parsley, it will not get much in the way of outside help. I like Charlottes, with their hint of sweetness, for this simple recipe.

2 1/2 pounds small Charlotte potatoes, peeled
2 tablespoons unsalted butter
2 tablespoons finely minced fresh flat-leaf parsley
Salt and freshly ground black pepper

Place the potatoes in a saucepan of salted water to cover, bring to a boil, decrease the heat to a simmer, and cook for about 20 minutes, until the potatoes are tender. Drain the potatoes and return them to the saucepan.

Add the butter to the saucepan and roll the potatoes in it until it melts. Add the parsley, gently toss the potatoes, season with salt and pepper, and serve at once.

German Butterball

This potato is dynamite. As its name implies, it's a round, buttery-tasting customer not unlike Yukon Gold (page 92), but with rougher skin. It also has a fairly high starch content, making it fine for roasting or pan cooking. Most of the ones you'll find in American markets are small, but larger ones are excellent to shred for potato pancakes.

SUBSTITUTES: OZETTE, YELLOW FINN, YUKON GOLD

ROASTED POTATOES AND MUSHROOMS IN RED WINE VINAIGRETTE

YIELD: 4 SERVINGS

An inviting bundle of uniformly small, golden potatoes demands to be roasted. In this recipe, roasted German Butterballs are combined with wild mushrooms and nubbins of bacon in a warm red wine vinaigrette infused with shallots and strewn with parsley. It makes for an excellent first course or a delicious side dish with grilled or roasted chicken or beef. Though meaty, earthy-tasting mushrooms like porcini or blue foot are best, cremini can also be used. Plain white mushrooms will do as well, especially if they are not snow-white fresh and have been stored in an open basket and allowed to dry out and darken a bit, to deepen their flavor.

2 ounces slab bacon, diced

1 1/2 pounds small German Butterball potatoes, scrubbed and halved

Salt and freshly ground black pepper

2/3 cup dry red wine

3 shallots, finely chopped

1/2 cup extra virgin olive oil

20 medium-small exotic mushrooms (porcini, blue foot, or cremini), halved

4 tablespoons unsalted butter

1/2 cup loosely packed small flat-leaf parsley sprigs

Preheat the oven to 400°.

Place a nonstick skillet over medium heat, add the bacon, and sauté until lightly browned. Remove the bacon, leaving the fat in the pan. Add the potatoes to the skillet and sauté, moving them around, for about 10 minutes, until they start to brown. Season with salt and pepper. Arrange the potatoes in a single layer in a baking dish and roast for about 30 minutes, until tender and well browned.

Meanwhile, place the wine in a saucepan and cook over high heat until reduced to 3 tablespoons. Cool briefly, then mix in the shallots, 1/3 cup of the olive oil, and salt and pepper to taste to form a vinaigrette. Set aside.

When the potatoes are nearly done, add the remaining olive oil to the skillet over high heat and brown the mushrooms for about 2 minutes on each side. Add the butter and parsley and fry for another minute. Fold in the roasted potatoes. Season to taste with salt and pepper.

Warm the vinaigrette briefly. Transfer the potatoes and mushrooms to a serving dish, stir the vinaigrette, pour over the vegetables, and serve.

Ozette

This potato brings a bit of history. The name is that of a Native American tribe of Washington's Olympic Peninsula. As the story goes, Spaniards brought the ancestors of the Ozette from Peru to California and then on up to Washington, where they traded the potatoes with the local tribe. They're now sometimes called Ozette Indian. Although these elongated, knobby ovals with thin skin and a toasty flavor are grown mainly in Washington, farmers—and shoppers—elsewhere have discovered them. They boil up dry and starchy, making them candidates for recipes with some fat in them.

SUBSTITUTES: GERMAN BUTTERBALL, PAPA AMARILLA, YELLOW FINN, YUKON GOLD

PAPAS A LA HUANCAINA

(PERUVIAN POTATOES
WITH CHEESE)

YIELD: 8 APPETIZER SERVINGS

This Peruvian classic is perhaps the best way to showcase potatoes in a recipe from their country of origin. In Cuzco, the ancient Incan capital of Peru, I was usually served the dish cold, on an iceberg-lettuce-lined platter with lavish garnishes of olives, eggs, corn, and onions. It's essentially a potato salad with a sumptuously creamy cheese sauce. I've adapted the recipe somewhat, substituting an underpinning of arugula for the iceberg lettuce, using fresh corn kernels instead of slices of corn on the cob, and presenting it warm, for a rich, lovely first course to serve as a prelude for a simple main dish such as grilled fish. If Ozettes are not available, Yukon Golds (page 92), Papa Amarillas (page 79), or even Long Whites (page 40) can be used.

1/4 cup freshly squeezed lime juice

1/8 teaspoon pure chile powder, or to taste

Salt and freshly ground black pepper

1 red onion, thinly sliced and separated into rings

10 medium Ozette potatoes (about 2 pounds)

2 ears corn

3 cups coarsely chopped fairly bland white cheese
    (Mexican *queso blanco*, Monterey Jack, or
    processed Muenster)

1 long fresh red or yellow chile, seeded
    and chopped

3/4 teaspoon ground turmeric

1 1/2 cups heavy cream

1 tablespoon extra virgin olive oil

2 bunches arugula, stemmed, rinsed,
    and dried

4 hard-cooked eggs, quartered, for garnish

8 oil-cured black olives, for garnish

8 small sprigs cilantro, for garnish

In a bowl, combine the lime juice and chile powder. Season with salt and pepper to taste and add the onion rings. Set aside to marinate.

Place the potatoes in a saucepan, cover with cold water, bring to a boil, decrease the heat to a simmer, and cook for about 20 minutes, until tender. Transfer the potatoes with a slotted spoon to a large bowl and cover with a damp towel to keep warm. Place the corn in the liquid remaining in the saucepan and boil for 2 minutes. Drain. When the cobs are cool enough to handle, strip the kernels from them. You should have about 2/3 cup kernels.

In a blender or food processor, combine the cheese, chile, turmeric, and cream and process until smooth. Heat the olive oil in a heavy nonstick skillet, add the cheese mixture, and cook over low heat, stirring constantly, until the sauce is smooth. Fold in the corn kernels. Season to taste with salt and pepper.

Arrange the arugula on a serving platter or on each of 8 salad plates. Slice the potatoes 1/2 inch thick, season lightly with salt and pepper, and arrange them on the arugula. Pour the cheese sauce over the potato slices and spread the onion rings on top. Garnish with the egg wedges, olives, and cilantro and serve.

BACON-POTATO CAKE

YIELD: 8 SERVINGS

Mahogany strips of smoky bacon wrap the potatoes in this decadent dish that Andrew Chase, the chef at the Monkey Bar in Manhattan, serves alongside steak. Truly, you do not need the steak and can just serve the potato cake with a green salad for brunch. Left unmolded, the cake can be set aside when it's finished, then reheated in the oven for 20 minutes before serving. If nutty-tasting Ozette potatoes are not available, Long Whites (page 40) or even Russets (page 48) can be substituted.

1 tablespoon unsalted butter
3 pounds Ozette potatoes, peeled and thinly sliced
Salt and freshly ground black pepper
6 ounces slab bacon, thinly sliced
1/2 pound Gruyère cheese, shredded

Preheat the oven to 425°. Use the butter to grease a 10-inch cast-iron skillet.

Pat the potatoes dry on paper towels, place them in a bowl, and season with salt and pepper.

Line the skillet with the bacon slices, starting each slice at the middle of the pan and arranging them like the spokes of a wheel, slightly overlapping. Allow the ends to hang over the edges of the pan.

Arrange one-third of the potatoes in the pan. Top with half of the cheese. Add half the remaining potatoes, the rest of the cheese, and the rest of the potatoes. Fold the overhanging ends of the bacon back over the top. Place in the oven and bake for about 45 minutes, until the potatoes offer no resistance when pierced with the point of a sharp knife. Use a spatula to compress the cake a few times during baking.

Allow the skillet to cool on a rack for a few minutes. Place a large plate upside down over the skillet and invert to unmold the cake. Cut into wedges and serve.

Papa Amarilla

The name leaves little doubt as to the South American origin of this potato. It's starchy and rich-tasting, with a rounded, slightly uneven shape and golden skin that often blushes purple. The newfound interest in interpreting Hispanic food has created a bit of demand for this rare and unusual potato, especially from chefs. Some growers are experimenting with hybrids and new strains, giving them names like Mama Amarilla and Inca Gold. (Papa Amarillas themselves are so rare that Inca Golds are shown here.) They can be sautéed, used in salads, and, after parboiling, stir-fried.

SUBSTITUTES: OZETTE, YELLOW FINN, YUKON GOLD

CORN AND POTATO CHOWDER

YIELD: 6 SERVINGS

It's hard to imagine a chowder without potatoes. Milky clam chowder derives its thickening from the starchy potatoes simmered with the clams. In this recipe, corn vies with the potatoes to be the center of attention in a lightly spiced mixture enhanced with a confetti of sweet red peppers. Floury, bright gold Papa Amarillas suit this chowder to perfection, but they're not easy to find, so the reliable Yukon Gold (page 92) makes a fine substitute.

1 tablespoon unsalted butter

1 cup finely chopped onion

1/2 cup finely chopped red bell pepper

1 teaspoon ground cumin

1/4 teaspoon cayenne pepper, or to taste

1 pound Papa Amarilla potatoes, peeled and diced

4 cups lowfat milk

2 cups fresh corn kernels (from about 6 ears)

Salt and freshly ground black pepper

2 tablespoons minced fresh cilantro

Melt the butter in a heavy saucepan over low heat. Add the onion and bell pepper and cook slowly for about 6 minutes, until the vegetables are tender. Stir in the cumin and cayenne pepper.

Add the potatoes and milk to the saucepan. Bring to a simmer, cover, and cook for about 20 minutes, until the potatoes are tender. Remove from the heat and, using a fork, coarsely mash most of the potatoes in the pot.

Stir in the corn, bring to a simmer, and cook for 5 minutes, until the corn is tender. Season to taste with salt and pepper. Stir in the cilantro and serve.

Peanut

As its name implies, this is a tiny potato, a teardrop-shaped fingerling with brownish, somewhat rough-textured skin. Sometimes it's called Spanish Peanut. Its flesh is dark gold, dense, and a bit starchy, permitting it to absorb the flavors of a sauce. It will hold up well if added to a braised dish or stew, and is also good roasted. But don't try to peel the Peanut unless you have hours to spare and patience for tedium.

SUBSTITUTES: AUSTRIAN CRESCENT, GERMAN BUTTERBALL, SMALL RATTE, RUSSIAN BANANA, YELLOW FINN

PEANUT POTATOES AND STEAK
WITH ASIAN MARINADE

YIELD: 4 SERVINGS

No, I could not resist using peanuts to season a dish made with Peanut potatoes. This is meat and potatoes with Southeast Asian flair. The steak is marinated in a peanut butter mixture and the potatoes, sautéed with shallots and ginger, are bathed in a sauce made from the same ingredients and served over the sliced steak. If you can't find small Peanut potatoes, use other fingerlings, like Austrian Crescent (page 62), Russian Banana (page 87), or French Fingerling (page 104), but be sure to cut them in small pieces.

2 tablespoons plus 1 1/2 teaspoons unsalted creamy
    peanut butter

Juice of 1 lime

2 tablespoons soy sauce

1 (1 3/4-pound) flank steak

2 tablespoons peanut oil

1 1/4 pounds Peanut potatoes, scrubbed and
    cut into 1-inch pieces

1/4 cup thinly sliced shallot

1 teaspoon finely minced fresh ginger

1 cup beef stock

Pinch of crushed red pepper flakes

1 scallion, trimmed and minced

1 tablespoon minced fresh cilantro

2 tablespoons chopped salted peanuts

Place the peanut butter in a small bowl. Gradually whisk in the lime juice until the mixture is smooth. Stir in the soy sauce.

Place the steak in a shallow glass or ceramic dish. Pour 2 tablespoons of the peanut butter mixture over the meat and rub in on both sides. Cover and refrigerate for about 3 hours.

Heat the oil in a skillet over medium heat. Add the potatoes and sauté, stirring occasionally, for about 10 minutes, until they start to soften and take on color. Add the shallot and ginger and continue to sauté for another 8 to 10 minutes, until the potatoes are nearly cooked through. Stir in the stock and the remaining marinade, decrease the heat to low, and simmer until the mixture reduces somewhat and a saucelike consistency forms. Season to taste with the pepper flakes, cover, and remove from the heat.

Preheat a grill or broiler to very hot. In a small bowl, combine the scallion, cilantro, and peanuts and set aside.

Grill or broil the steak close to the source of heat, turning once, for 3 to 4 minutes per side, until seared and medium-rare. Remove from the heat, slice thin on the diagonal against the grain, and arrange the slices on a serving platter.

Briefly reheat the potato mixture over low heat. Pour it over and around the steak, scatter the peanut mixture on top, and serve.

Ratte

The Chanel of potatoes, the Ratte, or La Ratte, as some would have it, is the French designer potato par excellence. It's a favorite of French chefs and has started attracting attention on this side of the Atlantic. In France, Rattes are grown to a fairly generous size, but American farmers are keeping their ovals on the small side, making it more difficult to use the creamy, pale gold flesh with its suggestion of hazelnuts and chestnuts in dishes that require peeled potatoes. The Ratte can be grown as a fingerling, but not necessarily so. It's a lovely all-purpose potato, just as superb in a buttery purée as sautéed. Sometimes it is sold under the name "Princess." Like the Bintje (page 64), however, the Ratte is a European potato that seems destined to become more widely available in the States.

SUBSTITUTES: CHARLOTTE, RUSSIAN BANANA, YUKON GOLD

BRAISED CHICKEN AND POTATOES

YIELD: 4 SERVINGS

Braised baby chickens nesting among creamy potatoes for sopping up the delicious wine-enriched juices make a splendid main dish for an intimate dinner. Fingerling or oval potatoes, like Ratte or Russian Banana (page 87), would be my choice. Try to select ones of uniform size, not just for appearance, but so they'll cook evenly.

4 poussins (baby chickens) or Cornish hens

Salt and freshly ground black pepper

Several thyme sprigs

Several rosemary sprigs

1 1/2 tablespoons unsalted butter

2 tablespoons minced shallots

2 cloves garlic, minced

1/2 cup dry white wine

1/2 cup well-flavored chicken stock

2 pounds Ratte potatoes, peeled

Juice of 1/2 lemon

1 tablespoon chopped fresh flat-leaf parsley

Rinse and dry the chickens inside and out. Season the cavities with salt and pepper. Slip some of the herbs into the cavities. Tuck the wing tips to the back of the birds and tie the legs with butcher's cord.

Over medium-high heat, melt 1/2 tablespoon of the butter in a heavy ovenproof casserole large enough to hold the chickens. Brown the chickens on all sides on top of the stove. Remove them from the casserole.

Preheat the oven to 400°.

Add the shallots to the butter remaining in the casserole and sauté over medium heat for about 4 minutes, until tender and beginning to color. Add the garlic, cook

continued

briefly, then stir in the wine and stock. Remove from the heat. Place the chickens in the casserole, cover, and place in the oven for 25 minutes.

Meanwhile, place the potatoes in a saucepan, cover with salted water, bring to a boil, decrease the heat to a simmer, and cook for about 20 minutes, until just tender.

When the chickens are done, transfer them to a warmed serving platter. Place the casserole on top of the stove and add the potatoes. Simmer gently for about 5 minutes, turning the potatoes in the sauce. Season to taste with salt and pepper. Add the lemon juice and any juices from the chickens on the platter, then swirl in the remaining 1 tablespoon butter bit by bit.

Remove the trussing and herbs from the chickens. Arrange the chickens on the platter and spoon the sauce and potatoes around them. Sprinkle with the parsley before serving.

Russian Banana

The name of this potato sounds like some kind of joke. But it's a fingerling, supposedly of Russian origin and now cultivated in the Pacific Northwest and the Northeast. The banana part is descriptive of its shape and color. As a category, fingerlings are just starting to achieve recognition in America. For that reason, why not show them off in recipes in which they're roasted, boiled, or sautéed whole? As fingerlings go, the Russian Banana is relatively easy to find in specialty markets. It has thin ivory-beige skin, straw-colored flesh, and a rich, true potato taste with that hint of sweetness typical of the gold group.

SUBSTITUTES: AUSTRIAN CRESCENT, CAROLA, PEANUT, RATTE

BRAISED MONKFISH WITH POTATOES AND MELTED LEEKS

YIELD: 4 SERVINGS

This recipe is an adaptation of one of the signature dishes that Gilbert Le Coze, a founder of Le Bernardin in Paris, then New York, created for the restaurant. The difference is the addition of the potatoes to make it a one-dish main course. I like to use bold-tasting Russian Bananas, but other small fingerlings are also suitable.

1 tablespoon extra virgin olive oil

2 ounces slab bacon, diced

3 tablespoons finely chopped shallots

2 bunches leeks, white part only, rinsed
    and chopped

1 tablespoon minced fresh chives

2/3 cup dry white wine

1 pound Russian Banana potatoes, scrubbed

1 1/2 pounds monkfish fillet, cut into
    1-inch-thick slices

Juice of 1/2 lemon

Salt and freshly ground black pepper

Heat the oil in a heavy 3-quart casserole over medium heat. Add the bacon and sauté until it starts to brown. Add the shallots and leeks and sauté over low heat for about 4 minutes, until softened but not brown. Stir in half of the chives. Add half of the wine and stir, scraping the bottom of the pan. Arrange the potatoes on top of the leeks. Cover and cook over low heat for about 25 minutes, until the leeks are very soft and the potatoes are tender. Remove from the heat.

Add the remaining wine to the casserole and bring to a simmer. Place the slices of monkfish on top of the leeks and potatoes, season with salt and pepper, cover the casserole, and cook over low heat for about 10 minutes, until the fish is just done. Add the lemon juice, adjust the seasoning if needed, dust with the remaining chives, and serve.

Yellow Finn

The Yellow Finn is a close cousin to the Yukon Gold, only starchier and more flavorful. It has a rich, buttery taste and is grown in the Pacific Northwest, California, and New York. I've used Yellow Finns to make out-of-the-ordinary baked potatoes with excellent results, but their considerable starch content also puts them high on the list of potatoes for a gratin.

SUBSTITUTES: GERMAN BUTTERBALL, YUKON GOLD

GRATIN OF POTATOES AND ASPARAGUS

YIELD: 6 SERVINGS

A starchy potato works best in potato gratins like this one, which combines potatoes and asparagus and is finished with Parmigiano-Reggiano cheese. When I plan to make this potato gratin, I look for Yellow Finns. But a Russet of some kind (page 48) would do just fine. You can substitute half-and-half for some or all the milk, or even replace a cup of it with heavy cream to enrich this suave preparation.

3 tablespoons unsalted butter
2 pounds Yellow Finn potatoes, peeled and sliced
4 cloves garlic, smashed
3 1/2 cups milk
Salt and freshly ground black pepper
1/2 pound slender asparagus, ends snapped off and
    spears cut into 1-inch pieces
1/4 cup freshly grated Parmigiano-Reggiano cheese

Preheat the oven to 375°. Butter a 2-quart shallow baking dish with 1 tablespoon of the butter.

Combine the potatoes, garlic, and milk in a heavy saucepan. Bring to a simmer and cook for 10 minutes. Season to taste with salt and pepper.

Spoon half of the mixture into the prepared baking dish. Scatter the asparagus over the potatoes, then top with the remaining potato mixture. Dot with the remaining 2 tablespoons butter and sprinkle with the cheese.

Bake for about 45 minutes, until golden brown on top, then serve.

SILKEN POTATO PURÉE

There's no point in cutting corners if your goal is a potato purée that's pure satin. This is not a dish for dieters. Copious amounts of butter and cream are needed to smooth the way. But when you serve such a purée to dinner guests, the raves are guaranteed. What makes this purée unusual is that it calls for a mixture of potatoes, Yellow Finns and Russets, something that Georges Perrier, chef and owner of Le Bec Fin in Philadelphia, has suggested. If Yellow Finns are not in the market, look for Rattes (page 84) or at least Yukon Golds (page 92).

4 large Yellow Finn potatoes, peeled
    and cut into eighths
2 large Russet potatoes, peeled and cut into eighths
1 cup heavy cream
1/4 cup to 1/2 cup unsalted butter, cut into pieces
Salt and freshly ground black pepper

Place the potatoes in a saucepan, cover with cold water, bring to a boil, decrease the heat to a simmer, and cook for about 20 minutes, until the potatoes are quite tender. Drain the potatoes and return them to the saucepan. Cook them over medium heat for a few minutes, moving them around with a wooden spoon, until they are dry.

In a separate saucepan, heat the cream over medium heat until small bubbles appear along the edges of the pan.

Remove the potatoes from the saucepan, then force them through a ricer back into the saucepan. Stir in the cream and add the butter to taste, bit by bit. Season to taste with salt and pepper. Reheat if necessary and serve hot.

Yukon Gold

Like arugula in a salad bowl and balsamic vinegar in a dressing, Yukon Golds, virtually unknown before the 1990s, have taken over the market, satisfying consumers hungry for a change of pace from everyday white potatoes. The Yukon Gold was developed in Canada in the early 1980s, hence the name. It grows round or slightly elongated and has fairly smooth yellow flesh and skin and distinctive pinkish eyes. It has become a staple, the new all-purpose potato, grown on both coasts and widely sold in supermarkets. Unlike many of the newer varieties, farmers are harvesting larger sizes, not just small ones. Some markets sell generic gold potatoes, which are not Yukons but come close. Is it the yellow color, suggesting a buttery taste, that explains their appeal?

SUBSTITUTES: GERMAN BUTTERBALL, YELLOW FINN

GARLICKY MASHED POTATOES

The secret to making good mashed potatoes? Use a potato ricer to do the mashing and heat the milk before adding it. If need be, you could mash potatoes with a fork or with one of those utensils that crushes the potatoes with a heavy zigzag wire, but neither one is as effective as a ricer. Under no circumstances should you attempt to mash potatoes in a food processor. The result will be a gluey mass. As for which kind of potato makes the best mashed? The current consensus is the medium- to high-starch Yukon Gold, which seems to have a buttery quality all its own. These mashed potatoes are seasoned with what might seem like an abundance of garlic. But the garlic has been tamed by simmering it with the potatoes, instead of using it raw.

3 pounds large Yukon Gold potatoes, peeled and
cut into 2-inch uniform chunks
6 cloves garlic, peeled but left whole
3/4 cup milk
Salt and freshly ground black pepper
1 to 6 tablespoons unsalted butter, at room
temperature, or 2 tablespoons extra virgin
olive oil

Place the potatoes and garlic in a saucepan, cover with cold water, bring to a boil, decrease the heat to medium, and simmer for about 20 minutes, until the potatoes are tender.

In a separate small saucepan, heat the milk over medium heat until small bubbles appear along the edges of the pan.

Drain the potatoes and garlic and mash together, preferably using a ricer. Return the potatoes to the saucepan and add the hot milk, fluffing the potatoes with a fork. Season to taste with salt and pepper. Add the desired amount of butter and serve at once.

CHILE-SPICED POTATOES

YIELD: 6 SERVINGS

Although rice is most frequently the starch of choice with Southwestern and Mexican dishes, these potatoes, zapped with a bolt of jalapeño, provide suitably forceful flavors alongside barbecued meats, spice-rubbed grilled chicken or prawns, or even brunch-time huevos rancheros. Large Yukon Golds work fine in this recipe, but it's also worth considering sweet potatoes (page 132). This dish is also good cold, a kind of spicy potato salad to take on a picnic, especially with some sour cream folded in.

3 pounds large Yukon Gold potatoes, peeled
   and cut into 1-inch dice
1/4 cup extra virgin olive oil
2 red onions, chopped
2 jalapeño chiles, seeded and minced
2 teaspoons ground cumin
1/2 teaspoon pure chile powder, or to taste
Salt
1/4 cup minced fresh cilantro

Place the potatoes in a saucepan, add cold salted water to cover, bring to a boil, and decrease the heat to a simmer; parboil for 10 minutes. They will be undercooked. Drain.

Heat the olive oil in a large nonstick skillet over medium heat. Add the potatoes and sauté for about 10 minutes, until they are barely beginning to take on color. Stir in the onions, jalapeños, cumin, and chile powder and continue to sauté for another 10 minutes, until the onions are tender and the potatoes are lightly browned. Season to taste with salt, fold in the cilantro, and serve.

FARFALLE WITH POTATOES, ARTICHOKES, AND MUSHROOMS

Like the Pizzoccheri Casserole on page 68, this is a pasta recipe that includes potatoes. The trick here is that the potatoes and artichokes are cooked together, and the pasta is then added to the same pot. Talk about convenience. Tiny potatoes, like the little Yukon Golds that are easily found these days, are best. Don't use a red-skinned potato, however. It just looks wrong.

1 pound baby artichokes

Juice of 1 lemon

1 pound very small Yukon Gold potatoes, scrubbed and halved

1 pound farfalle (bow-tie pasta)

3 tablespoons extra virgin olive oil

1/2 pound fresh cremini or white mushrooms, sliced

2 cloves garlic, thinly sliced

1/2 cup chicken or mushroom stock

1 tablespoon soy sauce

Salt and freshly ground black pepper

1 tablespoon slivered fresh basil

Freshly grated Parmigiano-Reggiano cheese

Bring a large pot of salted water to a boil. Meanwhile, trim the artichokes: Slice off 1/2 inch of the tops, then slice the stem flush with the bottom. Pull off 2 or 3 outer layers of leaves, quarter what's left lengthwise, and remove the prickly interior leaves and fuzz. As they are trimmed, toss the artichokes in a bowl with the lemon juice.

When the water is boiling, add the artichokes and potatoes, decrease the heat to a simmer, and cook for about 10 minutes, until both are nearly tender. Add the farfalle, raise the heat to high, and boil for 8 minutes, until everything is just tender. Drain the contents of the pot, leaving some moisture clinging to the ingredients.

continued

Heat the olive oil in a very large skillet over medium-high heat. Add the mushrooms and garlic and sauté for about 6 minutes, just until the mushrooms have wilted. Add the artichokes, potatoes, and farfalle to the skillet along with the stock and soy sauce. Stir around briefly, then season to taste with salt and pepper.

Transfer to a large serving bowl, sprinkle with the basil and cheese, and serve.

POTATO AND ALMOND CAKE

YIELD: 8 SERVINGS

In the event that you're considering serving an all-potato menu, here's the dessert you'll need. It's adapted from a recipe created by New York chef Daniel Boulud. Poached pears are delicious alongside it.

4 tablespoons unsalted butter, plus extra for
    pan preparation
2 1/2 tablespoons all-purpose flour, plus extra
    for pan preparation
1/2 teaspoon baking powder
2/3 cup sugar
2 egg whites
1 cup mashed Yukon Gold potatoes, cooled
2 tablespoons heavy cream
1 teaspoon vanilla extract
3 egg yolks
1/4 cup sliced blanched almonds

Preheat the oven to 400°. Butter an 8-inch springform pan, dust with flour, and shake out the excess.

Whisk together the flour, baking powder, and 2 tablespoons of the sugar in a bowl. Set aside. Melt the remaining butter and reserve.

In another bowl, beat the egg whites until they form soft peaks. While beating constantly, gradually add all but 1 tablespoon of the remaining sugar, until the whites are firm and glossy. Set aside.

In a large bowl, whisk the mashed potatoes with the melted butter, cream, vanilla, and egg yolks until smooth. Stir in the reserved flour mixture. Fold in the beaten egg whites until fairly well incorporated. Pour the batter into the prepared pan and smooth the top. Sprinkle evenly with the almonds and the reserved 1 tablespoon sugar.

Place in the oven and bake for about 20 minutes, rotating the pan halfway through, until the cake is golden brown, shrinking from the sides of the pan a bit, and springy to the touch. Cool on a rack, remove the sides of the pan, and serve.

RED
POTATOES

Unlike the golds, where the flesh is the defining component, red potatoes are identified by their skin color. Some do have pinkish to red flesh but more are snowy white. They come small and large, usually round, and occasionally fingerling. Most appear in the market soon after harvesting, making them what are generally called "new" potatoes, with relatively thin skins and low-starch, waxy textures.

All Red

The beauty of the All Red is more than skin deep. It's red through and through, from its deep magenta skin to its stunning pink flesh. But the flavor does not quite match the visual allure, because the potato is on the bland side. It comes in a medium-sized oval with flesh that's waxy and quite moist, making it an excellent candidate for a well-seasoned salad in a mayonnaise dressing.

SUBSTITUTES: RED BLISS

HERBED POTATO SALAD

Almost a classic, this potato salad in a creamy mayonnaise dressing is bolstered with garlic and herbs. When made with All Reds the color is stunning. But even unpeeled Red Bliss potatoes (page 107) can be used to handsome effect.

1 1/2 pounds All Red potatoes, peeled
3 tablespoons red wine vinegar
1 tablespoon chopped shallots
1 small clove garlic, minced
1/2 cup mayonnaise
1 tablespoon Dijon mustard
2 tablespoons extra virgin olive oil
1 1/2 teaspoons drained small capers
1 tablespoon finely minced fresh tarragon
1 tablespoon finely minced fresh flat-leaf parsley
1 tablespoon minced fresh chervil
Salt and freshly ground black pepper

Place the potatoes in a saucepan with cold salted water to cover, bring to a boil, decrease the heat to a simmer, and cook for about 20 minutes, until just tender. Drain and immediately toss with 2 tablespoons of the vinegar. Allow to cool, then slice 1/4 inch thick. Place in a bowl. Fold in the shallots and garlic.

In a separate bowl, mix together the mayonnaise, mustard, remaining 1 tablespoon vinegar, olive oil, capers, and herbs. Pour the dressing over the potatoes and mix gently. Season to taste with salt and pepper and serve.

Desirée

This is a pretty potato, a near-perfect oval with thin, rose-tinted golden skin and a fine-textured, creamy interior that holds its shape well. It's popular in Europe and no wonder: It's as versatile as our Yukon Gold. Simply steamed or boiled, the delicate, almost fruity flavor of Desirées comes through nicely. But they're also wonderful brushed with olive oil, strewn with rosemary and coarse salt, and roasted whole. Because they slice exceptionally well after cooking, they're superb in salads and sautés.

SUBSTITUTES: FRENCH FINGERLING, RED BLISS, RUBY CRESCENT

MUSSEL AND POTATO SALAD

YIELD: 4 SERVINGS

I find potato salad to be irresistible. I love it so many different ways—mixed with a creamy mayonnaise, a vinaigrette, a yogurt dressing. And because I could make a meal of potato salad, I devised a recipe for it that results in a dish substantial enough to be a main course for a summer lunch. Mussels and potatoes with small tomatoes and olives prove a felicitous mix of flavors in a colorful display. Waxy Desirée potatoes are tailor-made for this salad.

1/2 pound small Desirée potatoes, peeled

1/4 cup white wine vinegar

1 tablespoon Dijon mustard

1 teaspoon anchovy paste

1/2 cup extra virgin olive oil

2 cloves garlic, minced

48 mussels, steamed open, chilled, and shucked

1 pint cherry tomatoes, stemmed and quartered

12 tiny niçoise olives, pitted

1 tablespoon minced fresh flat-leaf parsley

1 teaspoon freshly grated orange zest

Salt and freshly ground black pepper

Place the potatoes in a saucepan, cover with cold water, bring to a boil, decrease the heat to a simmer, and cook for 15 minutes, until just tender. Drain and allow to cool briefly, then slice the potatoes. Place in a bowl.

In a small bowl, mix the vinegar with the mustard and anchovy paste. Slowly whisk in the olive oil until emulsified, then stir in the garlic. Pour over the potatoes and toss gently. Fold in the mussels, tomatoes, olives, parsley, and orange zest. Season to taste with salt and pepper and serve.

French Fingerling

One of the newer varieties in the rapidly expanding fingerling category is called the French Fingerling, in a nod to the ancestry of the seed stock. It's a plump elongated oval with a smooth red skin and light yellow flesh mottled and streaked with red that has a silky texture and a rich flavor with a hint of mineral. The starch content is medium to low, making it a lovely candidate to incorporate whole in recipes that give it a chance to absorb a sauce without falling apart.

SUBSTITUTES: AUSTRIAN CRESCENT, RUBY CRESCENT, RUSSIAN BANANA

RAGOUT OF NEW POTATOES AND SPRING VEGETABLES

YIELD: 8 SERVINGS

The notion of early crop potatoes, as they are called in England, or primeurs *as they are known in France, has not taken hold in America. In those countries, certain varieties—potatoes that are as much a harbinger of spring as dewy fresh asparagus—are eagerly awaited, then treated with tender care when they arrive. The Bonnotte potato, of the French island of Noirmoutier, is a good example, and one that importers hope to make available soon—in limited quantities—to American chefs. Lacking these, small, smooth-skinned, nutty-tasting potatoes like the French Fingerling, the creamy Desirée (page 102), or even the more common Red Bliss (page 107), providing the skin is shiny, smooth, and taut, would be fine to anchor and provide substance to this light, but elegant, vegetable ragout. It deserves a final drizzle of truffle oil, but it is lovely even without that bit of indulgence.*

2 pounds small French Fingerling potatoes, scrubbed

1/4 pound tiny pearl onions, skin on

1/2 pound green beans, ends trimmed

1 pound very slender asparagus, ends snapped off

1 pound baby carrots, peeled

1/2 pound snow peas or sugar snap peas, ends trimmed

3 tablespoons extra virgin olive oil

2 bunches scallions, chopped

1/2 cup well-flavored chicken stock

Salt and freshly ground black pepper

1 tablespoon finely minced fresh chives

1 tablespoon black truffle oil (optional)

continued

If the potatoes are 1 1/2 inches in diameter or less, leave them whole. Otherwise, quarter them. Place them in a saucepan, cover with cold water, bring to a boil, decrease the heat to a simmer, and cook for about 20 minutes, until just tender. Drain and set aside.

Meanwhile, bring a saucepan full of water to a boil over high heat. Add the pearl onions and cook for 2 to 3 minutes, until slightly tender. Drain the onions, then cut off the root and stem ends. To free the onions from their skins, pinch each on one end—the peeled onion should pop out.

Slant-cut the green beans and asparagus into 1-inch lengths. Set aside.

In a separate saucepan, combine the carrots and onions with water to cover, bring to a boil, decrease the heat to medium, and simmer for 15 minutes, until just tender. With a slotted spoon, transfer to a plate and set aside. Add the green beans and peas to the simmering water and cook for 4 minutes, until just tender and bright green. Drain and rinse under cold running water to halt the cooking. Drain and set aside.

About 10 minutes before serving, heat the olive oil in a large nonstick skillet over medium heat. Add the potatoes, carrots, and onions and sauté for about 5 minutes, until they barely begin to color. Stir in the green beans, peas, and asparagus and sauté for 2 to 3 minutes longer, until heated through and still bright green. Stir in the scallions and stock. Season to taste with salt and pepper, sprinkle with chives, and serve. Add a few drops of truffle oil to each portion at the last minute.

Red Bliss

Arguably the American standard-bearer of red-skinned potatoes, the Red Bliss is easy to come by and just as easy to use. Widely grown in California, it's not a boutique potato. Its skin is relatively thin and its ivory-white flesh is smooth and waxy—a classic salad potato.

SUBSTITUTES: CREAMER, DESIRÉE, FRENCH FINGERLING

DILLED POTATO SALAD

YIELD: 4 TO 6 SERVINGS

The best salad potatoes are low starch and waxy, so they stay coated with a dressing and do not become dry as the salad sits. The trick, then, is to coax them to absorb some of the dressing's flavor. For that, you begin when the potatoes are still hot, seasoning them with some of the vinegar and salt, then adding the rest of the dressing as they cool. The Red Bliss is an ideal salad potato, especially for salads that call for potatoes with the skin left on. This salad is dressed French style, with a vinaigrette.

2 pounds small Red Bliss potatoes, scrubbed
Salt and freshly ground black pepper
¹/₃ cup white wine vinegar
1 ¹/₂ teaspoons Dijon mustard
²/₃ cup extra virgin olive oil
¹/₄ cup chopped scallions
2 tablespoons minced fresh dill

Place the potatoes in a saucepan, cover with cold water, bring to a boil, cover, decrease the heat to low, and cook for about 20 minutes, until just tender. Drain the potatoes, then quarter them, taking care to keep the skins on.

Place the potatoes in a bowl, season lightly with salt and pepper, and gently toss with 2 tablespoons of the vinegar. Set aside to cool to room temperature.

In a small bowl, mix the remaining vinegar with the mustard until well blended. Slowly whisk in the olive oil until emulsified. Pour over the cooled potatoes and mix gently. Add the scallions and dill, season to taste with salt and pepper, and serve.

Red La Soda

L a Sodas have been around a long time but are relatively little known outside the Southeast, where they are grown. They are medium sized, round, and have smooth, rosy skins that tend to fade with time, so for fresher potatoes, look for those with good color. The flesh is pure white, with a low starch component at harvest and higher starch as they age.

SUBSTITUTES: RED BLISS

CREAMED LOBSTER HASH
WITH CAVIAR

YIELD: 4 SERVINGS

Leftover potatoes and corned beef, the remnants of a New England boiled dinner or a St. Patrick's Day celebration, combine to make corned beef hash. Roast beef or chicken frequently replace the corned beef. In this version, the humble hash becomes an aristocrat with lobster and caviar, giving it enough panache to make it worthy of being a first course for an elegant dinner party, even a

New Year's Eve celebration. The caviar is an optional luxury, but if you plan to use it, be sure it's high quality. Beluga is not necessary, but good, genuine American, Russian, or Iranian sturgeon roe is essential. Another option would be salmon or trout roe, or even a dusting of Japanese tobiko (flying fish roe). Red Blisses (page 107), Creamers (page 26), or Yukon Golds (page 92) can replace Red La Sodas in this recipe.

1 pound Red La Soda potatoes, peeled and diced

2 tablespoons unsalted butter

2 shallots, minced

3/4 cup finely chopped leek, white part only

1 1/2 cups diced cooked lobster meat
    (about 3/4 pound, or meat from two
    1-pound lobsters)

Juice of 1 lemon

4 teaspoons minced fresh tarragon, plus
    4 small sprigs

Salt and freshly ground black pepper

3/4 cup heavy cream or crème fraîche

4 slices fine-grained white bread, lightly toasted
    and crusts removed

2 ounces sturgeon caviar or salmon or trout roe
    (optional)

Place the potatoes in a saucepan, cover with salted cold water, bring to a boil, decrease the heat to a simmer, and cook for 8 to 10 minutes, until barely tender. Drain.

Melt the butter in a large nonstick skillet over medium heat. Add the potatoes and sauté for about 6 minutes, until they begin to color. Add the shallots and leeks and continue to sauté for about 2 minutes, until all the ingredients are golden. Fold in the lobster, lemon juice, and minced tarragon. Season to taste with salt and pepper. Add the cream and cook for several minutes, stirring gently, until the hash is heated through and the cream has thickened somewhat.

Place a slice of toast on each of 4 plates. Top with the lobster hash and a spoonful of the caviar. Garnish with tarragon sprigs.

Ruby Crescent

This rich tasting pinkish-skinned fingerling was long thought to be a different variety from the Rose Finn, or Rose Finn Apple, as it's sometimes called. Indeed, the first time I tried both, I thought they looked similar but did not taste the same. But it turns out that they are the same. My experience might have been the result of obtaining samples from markedly different soil, or possibly because the Ruby Crescents had been stored longer than the so-called Rose Finns.

Ruby Crescents are waxy, uneven fingerlings whose skin can be a bit chewy if the potato is not very fresh. The flesh is ivory to yellowish with a distinctive yeasty, almost milky flavor that intensifies as the potato cools. It's good to use in salads because the taste will not be submerged by a bold dressing, and it can also be sautéed with excellent results.

SUBSTITUTES: CREAMER, FRENCH FINGERLING, PEANUT

SKORDALIA

YIELD: 6 SERVINGS

As much as Americans adore mashed potatoes, the notion of using cold potato purée as the basis for a cocktail dip is not on the culinary radar screen. But there are some appetite-whetting examples, notably the brandade *of southern France, made with salt cod, and the Greek* skordalia, *a creamy potato and garlic mixture. Skordalia is by far the easier of the two to prepare. The dish is best made with a waxy-fleshed potato. The hint of cheese flavor that emerges as the Ruby Crescent cools makes it my choice, but Red Bliss (page 107) would also be fine. Be sure to use a very fruity extra virgin olive oil. This recipe has been adapted from the* skordalia *served at Estiatorio Milos in Manhattan.*

1 1/2 pounds Ruby Crescent potatoes, scrubbed
7 cloves garlic (about 1/4 cup)
1/3 cup extra virgin olive oil
2 tablespoons freshly squeezed lemon juice
Coarse sea salt
1/2 cup well-flavored fish stock or chicken stock
1 1/2 teaspoons minced fresh flat-leaf parsley
Toasted pita triangles or chips

Place the potatoes in a saucepan, cover with cold water, bring to a boil, decrease the heat to a simmer, and cook for about 15 minutes, until just tender. Do not overcook. They should still be a bit firm in the center. Drain the potatoes and, when cool enough to handle, peel them.

While the potatoes are cooking, pound the garlic in a mortar with 2 tablespoons of the olive oil, 2 teaspoons of the lemon juice, and a pinch of salt, to form a paste.

Transfer the mixture to a food processor or a heavy mixing bowl. Add 2 of the potatoes and process or mash them with the garlic mixture and some of the olive oil, lemon juice, salt, and stock. Continue adding the ingredients, reserving 1/2 tablespoon of the olive oil, to make a very smooth, creamy mixture.

Season to taste with additional salt if needed, transfer to a shallow dish, drizzle with the reserved oil, and sprinkle with the parsley. Serve with the pita triangles.

BLUE AND PURPLE POTATOES

Travel in the high Andes in Peru and you routinely come upon outdoor markets where the locals sell dozens of kinds of potatoes, the most arresting of which have deep purple to indigo skins. Blue and purple potatoes, grown mainly in the Northeast and California, are a recent addition in American specialty markets. At least one company is even producing purple potato chips.

All Blue

More blue than purple, the All Blue, a rounded or oval potato, is indeed blue through and through. Like most of the purple-blue varieties, it's starchy and sturdy, but it also has a slightly sweet flavor and a moist quality to its texture. Its thickish skin should be peeled before serving. Select it when color counts and when the recipe calls for marinating it in a sauce.

SUBSTITUTES: GERMAN BUTTERBALL, PURPLE PERUVIAN

POTATO CEVICHE

YIELD: 6 SERVINGS

Though ceviches are usually made with seafood, there are also a few vegetable ceviches, like this one in the South American style. Sturdy All Blues are excellent for it because they can withstand the relatively long marinating and still retain their character. It's important to allow the potatoes to cool completely before assembling the ceviche. The crunch of the daikon and peppers contrast the tender potatoes. And yes, there is a bit of seafood, some shrimp that are merely the garnish. There's also a nice trick with the shrimp: They're salted and allowed to sit a while, a technique used in Chinese cooking that improves the texture, firming it up. Try pre-salting your shrimp in other recipes, too.

2 pounds All Blue potatoes, scrubbed

1 red onion, diced

1 jalapeño chile, stemmed, seeded, and minced

1/2 cup diced green bell pepper

1/2 cup chopped fresh white radish (daikon)

4 scallions, finely chopped

2/3 cup freshly squeezed lime juice

18 medium shrimp (about 1/2 pound),
      peeled and deveined, for garnish

Salt

1/3 cup extra virgin olive oil

Freshly ground black pepper

3 tablespoons finely chopped fresh cilantro

6 lime wedges, for garnish

Place the potatoes in a saucepan, cover with cold water, bring to a boil, decrease the heat to a simmer, and cook for 15 to 20 minutes, until just barely tender. Do not overcook. Drain and allow to cool completely.

continued

Peel the potatoes and cut them into $1/2$-inch dice. Place in a bowl and mix in the onion, jalapeño, bell pepper, daikon, and scallions. Fold in the lime juice. Cover and allow to marinate, tossing once or twice, at room temperature for about 3 hours.

Meanwhile, toss the shrimp with 1 teaspoon salt and set aside for 30 minutes. Rinse and dry the shrimp. Heat 1 tablespoon of the oil in a heavy skillet or wok over high heat. Add the shrimp and stir-fry for 2 to 3 minutes, until just cooked through and lightly browned. Set aside until serving.

Season the potato mixture to taste with salt and pepper. Fold in the cilantro and remaining olive oil. Transfer to 6 stemmed goblets or martini glasses and garnish each serving with the shrimp and lime wedges.

Caribé

The skin can range from deep magenta-pink to purple, but the robust color is only skin deep. Unlike most blue and purple potatoes, the flesh of the Caribé is snow white. It delivers a rich flavor with a fairly starchy yet a bit waxy texture, making it an excellent choice for potato pancakes. And when left unpeeled, tiny flecks of color add a festive confetti note to the finished pancakes. Unpeeled Caribés also make terrific looking and tasting potato chips when sliced paper-thin.

SUBSTITUTES: RUSSET, YUKON GOLD

POTATO PANCAKE CANAPÉS WITH CAVIAR

YIELD: 16 TO 20 SMALL PANCAKES,
4 TO 6 SERVINGS

Grated potatoes mixed with onion, egg, and flour or matzoh meal is the basic formula for latkes, one of the standards of the Jewish kitchen. If you use potatoes with relatively thin skins and scrub them well first, it's not necessary to peel them. But a starchy variety, like Caribé, will yield the best results. Although the pancakes are best eaten as soon as they're fried, that's not the most practical approach, especially when you're entertaining with this dressy version. They can be kept warm in the oven for up to 30 minutes. The fallback, if Caribés are unavailable, is a Russet (page 48).

3 pounds large Caribé potatoes, unpeeled
1 onion
1 tablespoon freshly squeezed lemon juice
3 egg whites, lightly beaten
1 tablespoon minced fresh chives
3 tablespoons all-purpose flour or matzoh meal
Salt and freshly ground black pepper
About 3 tablespoons vegetable oil
1/2 cup sour cream or crème fraîche
4 ounces salmon roe or sturgeon caviar (optional)

Using the coarse plate of a box grater or food processor, grate the potatoes and the onion into a bowl. Mix in the lemon juice. Add the egg whites, chives, and flour. Season to taste with salt and pepper. (I actually season the raw mixture and taste it; otherwise, you can season and test by frying a little bit.)

Preheat the oven to 200°. Line a baking sheet with parchment paper.

Heat 1 tablespoon of the vegetable oil in a large, heavy nonstick skillet over medium heat. Working in batches, spoon tablespoons of the potato mixture into the skillet, flattening each lightly to make rounds 2 to 2 1/2 inches in diameter and 1/3 inch thick. Cook for about 5 minutes, until lightly browned on the underside. Turn and brown the other side for about 2 minutes. As the pancakes are done, transfer them to the baking sheet and place in the oven to keep warm. Repeat until all the batter is used, adding more oil to the pan as needed.

Serve the pancakes warm, topped with dollops of sour cream and caviar.

Purple Peruvian

This is a very high-starch, almost mealy textured potato with thick, shiny skin that must be peeled after cooking, and indigo flesh streaked with white. It's a medium-sized, oval potato with an assertive, earthy flavor and an inherent dryness that begs for a sauce. I find it best served cold, in a stunning salad.

SUBSTITUTES: ALL BLUE, ALL RED

PURPLE POTATO SALAD

YIELD: 8 SERVINGS

The intense, eye-catching color of this potato salad sets it apart. Although the potatoes of choice are often called Peruvian, the salad owes no particular allegiance to the intriguing cuisine of that country. Instead, it again proves how easily potatoes cross borders. For an inventive twist, consider preparing the salad with a mixture of purple or blue potatoes, All Reds (page 100), and snowy Creamers (page 26), and double or triple the recipe for a summer buffet. The color of the potatoes is more vibrant with this zesty vinaigrette dressing than it would be with a creamy mayonnaise. But could anything be more American than potato salad for the Fourth of July, and one that's red, white, and blue to boot?

3 pounds medium Purple Peruvian potatoes,
    scrubbed

2 tablespoons anchovy paste

1/4 cup red wine vinegar

3/4 cup extra virgin olive oil

2 to 3 jalapeño chiles, seeded and minced,
    or to taste

1 tablespoon finely grated lemon zest

Salt and freshly ground black pepper

1/2 cup finely chopped scallions

1/2 cup minced fresh mint

1/2 cup minced fresh flat-leaf parsley

Place the potatoes in a large saucepan, cover with cold water, bring to a boil, decrease the heat to a simmer, and cook for about 20 minutes, until just tender. Drain and allow to cool for about 30 minutes.

In a small bowl, dissolve the anchovy paste in a little of the vinegar, then stir in the remaining vinegar. Slowly whisk in the oil until emulsified, then fold in the jalapeños and lemon zest.

Peel the potatoes and slice them 1/3-inch thick. Place in a bowl and toss lightly with salt and pepper to taste. Pour the dressing over the potatoes, add the scallions, mint, and parsley, and toss again. Serve at once or set aside for up to 2 hours at room temperature before serving.

SWEET POTATOES

The Spaniards, traveling in the New World, are thought to have discovered the sweet potato before they encountered the white potato. Columbus came upon them in Hispaniola in 1492, and carried them back to Spain the following year. The Spanish name, *batata,* is sometimes used for the Boniato, the pale-fleshed subtropical sweet potato. What Americans think of as sweet potatoes—and market as yams—are the bold, moist orange-fleshed variety that was introduced in the South in the 1930s and became an instant hit. This book refers to them as sweet potatoes. A true yam is another tuber entirely and unrelated to the potato. It's nothing short of confusing.

Boniato

The Boniato deserves a wider audience in the United States. It's the classic sweet potato of the Caribbean and Central America, with pale ivory to orange flesh and a texture that is dryer than the so-called yam, as Americans generally call sweet potatoes. A variety called Red Garnet is closest to the American sweet potato. This somewhat knobby, misshapen tuber takes on a delicious caramelized flavor when baked.

SUBSTITUTES: HAYMAN SWEET

BONIATOS WITH BLACK BEANS

As has been noted, Boniatos deserve a bigger profile than they currently enjoy, in part because they can be used in place of the common Russet potato in a host of recipes. This dish, however, is adapted from a family recipe of Rafael Palomino, chef and owner of Sonora Restaurant in Manhattan, and it exploits the sweet potato's Hispanic connection. The mixture of black beans and white potatoes mashed together results in a violet shade that suggests the dish was made with purple potatoes. But the mellow Boniatos set it apart. Simmering the potatoes in chicken stock instead of water adds a rich dimension of flavor, and the roasted garlic provides a haunting depth to the sweetness to the dish.

4 large Boniatos, peeled and quartered

About 6 cups well-flavored chicken stock
    or vegetable stock

2 large cloves garlic, peeled but left whole

1/2 teaspoon olive oil

Salt

1 tablespoon unsalted butter, at room temperature

1/2 cup heavy cream, at room temperature

1 1/3 cups drained freshly cooked or canned
    black beans

1 tablespoon finely chopped fresh cilantro,
    for garnish

Preheat the oven to 350°.

Place the potatoes in a large saucepan and add the stock, making sure the potatoes are fully submerged. Bring to a boil and cook for about 25 minutes, until tender. Meanwhile, place the garlic in a piece of aluminum foil, moisten with the olive oil, and wrap loosely. Place in the oven for 15 minutes, or until the cloves are soft.

continued

Remove from the oven, discard the foil, and mash the garlic with a little salt.

When the potatoes are ready, drain them, return them to the saucepan, and mash by hand, adding the roasted garlic, salt to taste, butter, cream, and black beans. Beat until well mixed. Or, use an electric mixer to mash the sweet potatoes and beat in the other ingredients. Taste and adjust the seasonings.

Reheat the mashed potatoes in a saucepan over low heat and serve, garnished with the cilantro.

Hayman Sweet

Somehow in the era of New World discovery, the Caribbean sweet potato (Boniato, page 126) made its way to Virginia, possibly in the baggage of Spaniards who encountered the English, or even via Spain. Some historians think there might have been a native variety of sweet potato that grew in Virginia. Now, growers in Virginia have begun an aggressive program of cultivating Hayman Sweet, a strain of the Boniato, which they market under the name of Hayman Eastern Shore Selects. The medium-sized, irregular oval potatoes are pale ecru with a hint of gray and not particularly pretty, but their flavor is sweet and delicious without being cloying.

SUBSTITUTES: BONIATO, SWEET POTATO

CURRIED SWEET POTATO
PURÉE

YIELD: 6 TO 8 SERVINGS

Hayman Sweet, a "new" heirloom potato, is best for this recipe, especially since the curry powder enhances a potato that often turns grayish when cooked. But Boniatos (page 126) and regular sweet potatoes (page 132) would be fine choices, too, for this variation on mashed potatoes made by baking, not boiling, the spuds. The recipe may look long, but it's a casserole-style dish that can be prepared in advance, then given its final baking shortly before serving. Using yogurt adds a tangy, almost sweet-sour note to the potatoes.

**6 medium Hayman Sweet potatoes
(about 4 pounds total), scrubbed
2 tablespoons unsalted butter
1 tablespoon peeled and grated fresh ginger
1 tablespoon curry powder
1 cup plain yogurt, stirred
Salt and freshly ground black pepper**

Preheat the oven to 450°. Prick the sweet potatoes in 1 or 2 places with the tines of a fork or a skewer, place them on a baking sheet, and bake for about 50 minutes, until tender.

Meanwhile, melt 1 tablespoon of the butter in a large, heavy saucepan over medium heat. Stir in the ginger and cook for a few minutes, until fragrant. Add the curry powder and stir for another minute or so. Set aside to cool for 10 minutes, then stir in the yogurt. Set aside.

When the sweet potatoes have finished baking, remove them from the oven and decrease the oven temperature to 350°. Cut the potatoes in half horizontally and scoop the flesh out into a bowl. Discard the skins and mash the potatoes, using a potato masher or ricer, to make a smooth purée. Fold in the yogurt mixture. Season to taste with salt and pepper.

Brush a 4- to 6-cup baking dish with half of the remaining butter. Spread the purée in the dish and dot with the remaining butter. (The dish can be set aside for up to 2 hours before baking.)

Place the baking dish in the oven and bake for 20 minutes, until heated through. Serve at once.

Sweet Potato ("Yam")

The pointy oval, irregular tubers commonly called yams in the United States are actually a variety of Caribbean sweet potato. For the purposes of this book, I am considering only the deep orange to vermilion potatoes widely sold in markets and traditionally a part of Thanksgiving dinner. The potatoes range from mildly to extremely sweet, with very moist, sometimes slightly stringy flesh that mashes easily. They are rarely sold with their varietal names like Jewel, Garnet, and Hannah.

SUBSTITUTES: BONIATO, HAYMAN SWEET

BAKED SWEET POTATOES
AND APPLES

YIELD: 6 SERVINGS

You could probably divide the entire population of the United States into two camps: those who like marshmallows on their sweet potatoes and those who do not. Count me among the latter. Here is a different way to prepare sweet potatoes for your holiday table: baked and stuffed with apples and pecans and seasoned with ginger. Deep orange sweets are best for this recipe, but try to find potatoes that are uniform in size.

3 medium-large sweet potatoes (about 2 pounds), scrubbed

1 1/2 pounds tart apples, halved and cored

4 tablespoons unsalted butter

1 tablespoon peeled and minced fresh ginger

1 large shallot, minced

Salt and freshly ground black pepper

2 tablespoons finely chopped pecans

Preheat the oven to 400°. Line a baking sheet with aluminum foil.

Prick the sweet potatoes in 1 or 2 places with the tines of a fork or a skewer. Put the sweet potatoes on the prepared baking sheet and place in the oven. After 20 minutes, place the apples, cut side down, on the baking sheet. Continue baking for about 20 minutes, until the apples and potatoes are tender.

Meanwhile, melt the butter in a small sauté pan over low heat. Remove and reserve 1 tablespoon of it. Add the ginger and shallot to the butter remaining in the pan and sauté for about 5 minutes, until tender. Set aside.

When the sweet potatoes and apples are tender, remove from the oven and leave the oven set at 400°. Cut the potatoes in half horizontally and scoop the flesh out into

continued

a bowl. Reserve the skins. Peel the apples, discard the skins, and add the apples to the bowl. Mash the potatoes and apples together with a fork along with the ginger mixture. Season to taste with salt and pepper.

Pack the mixture back into the potato skins. (The stuffed potatoes can be set aside for up to 2 hours before baking.) Brush with the reserved melted butter and sprinkle with the pecans. Return them to the oven for about 15 minutes, to reheat and brown the tops.

SWEET POTATO-SQUASH PIE

YIELD: 6 SERVINGS

This recipe combines sweet potatoes and butternut squash for a new twist on an autumn pie. It's the perfect way to showcase the deep orange sweets commonly referred to as yams.

1 1/3 cups all-purpose flour, plus extra for rolling

1/2 teaspoon salt

6 tablespoons cold unsalted butter, diced,
      plus 2 tablespoons melted

About 4 tablespoons ice water

1 1/2 pounds sweet potatoes, cut into chunks

3 cups peeled and diced butternut squash

1/2 cup firmly packed light brown sugar

1/2 teaspoon freshly grated nutmeg

2 eggs, lightly beaten

1 teaspoon vanilla extract

1 cup heavy cream

2/3 cup chopped unsalted macadamia nuts

Preheat the oven to 425°.

Mix together the 1 1/3 cups flour and salt in a bowl. Cut in the cold butter using two knives or a pastry blender until the consistency of cornmeal. (Or combine the flour and salt in a food processor, add the butter, and pulse until like a coarse meal.) By hand, stir in the water, 1 tablespoon at a time, until the mixture can be gathered into a ball of dough.

Roll the dough out on a lightly floured surface and line a 9-inch pie pan with it. Prick the pastry in a couple of places with the tines of a fork, line it with aluminum foil, and fill with pastry weights or dried beans. Place in the oven and bake for 10 minutes. Remove the weights and foil and continue baking for about 15 minutes, until the pastry is lightly browned.

Meanwhile, combine the potatoes and squash in a saucepan, cover with lightly salted water, bring to a boil, decrease the heat to a simmer, and cook for about 30 minutes, until the vegetables are tender. Drain and pass the potatoes and squash through a ricer or a sieve placed over a bowl. Mix in the brown sugar, nutmeg, eggs, vanilla, and 1/3 cup of the cream.

Spread the purée in the baked pastry shell. Brush the top with the melted butter, and sprinkle with the nuts. Bake for about 30 minutes, until the top is lightly browned and the filling is set. Allow to cool on a rack, then refrigerate until serving.

Allow to come to room temperature before serving. Whip the remaining 2/3 cup cream and serve alongside.

Sources
for Potatoes

Though supermarkets are constantly expanding their potato inventories and specialty produce markets have become fine places to find boutique potatoes, the best way to obtain some of the more unusual varieties is by mail. In addition to mail-order catalogs, a number of farms and dealers now have websites, which provide detailed descriptions, and sometimes pictures, of the potatoes they offer. Some kinds are seasonal, sold in limited quantities, and not in stock at all times. Mid-summer to early winter is the best time to buy them, though advance orders may guarantee that you'll receive the ones you want when they're available.

When buying potatoes by mail, bear in mind that they will be very fresh, so it's important to use them—or share them with friends—soon after they arrive. Most companies ship overnight or second-day express. Be sure to check for minimum quantity requirements. Many, but not all, of the farms and distributors specialize in organically grown produce, so if this is important to you, be sure to verify that feature before you order.

A.V. THOMAS PRODUCE
(SWEET POTATOES)
P.O. Box 286
Livingston, CA 95334
800-654-0497 (800-433-7997 in California)

BOUCHEY POTATOES
(BOUTIQUE POTATOES)
2310 Evans Road
Wapito, WA 98951
509-848-2061
bouchey@televar.com

CROSSROAD FARMS
(BOUTIQUE POTATOES)
Indian River Crossroad
RR1 - Box 323
Jonesport, ME 04649
207-497-2641

CULINARY SPECIALTY PRODUCE
(BOUTIQUE POTATOES)
1190 Route 22 West
Mountainside, NJ 07092
908-789-4700
info@culinaryproduce.com

DIAMOND ORGANICS
(BOUTIQUE POTATOES)
P.O. Box 2159
Freedom, CA 95019
800-922-2396

GORANSON FARM
(ADVANCE ORDERS FOR EARLY POTATOES)
250 River Road (Route 128)
Dresden, ME 04342
207-737-8834
www.agate.net/~veggies/gfpotato.htm

HEIRLOOM HARVEST FARM
(BOUTIQUE POTATOES)
32 Pippin Hill Road
Blairstown, NJ 07825
908-362-9046

INDIAN ROCK PRODUCE
(BOUTIQUE AND SWEET POTATOES)
530 California Road
Quakertown, PA 18951
800-882-0512

Mountain Sweet Berry Farm
(boutique potatoes)
P.O. Box 667
Roscoe, NY 12776
607-498-4440
rnbishop@citlink.net

Rockey Farm
(boutique potatoes)
48284 County Road C
Center, CO 81125
719-754-3744

Ronniger's Organic Farm
(boutique and seed potatoes)
Star Route
Moyie Springs, ID 83845
888-267-7079

White Mountain Farm
(boutique potatoes)
8890 Lane 4 North
Mosca, CO 81146
800-364-3019

Wood Prairie Farm
(boutique potatoes, gift boxes)
49 Kinney Road
Bridgewater, ME 04735
800-829-9765
www.woodprairie.com

Bibliography

Conran, Caroline, Terence Conran, and Simon Hopkinson. *The Essential Cook Book.* New York: Stewart Tabori & Chang, 1997.

Davidson, Alan, ed. *The Oxford Companion to Food.* Oxford, England: Oxford University Press, 1999.

Fabricant, Florence. *New Home Cooking.* New York: Clarkson N. Potter, 1991.

Flandrin, Jean-Louis, and Massimo Montanari. *Food, A Culinary History.* Translated by Albert Sonnenfield. New York: Columbia University Press, 1999.

Fussell, Betty. *I Hear America Cooking.* New York: Viking, 1986.

Gabaccia, Donna R. *We Are What We Eat.* Cambridge: Harvard University Press, 1998.

Lang, Jenifer Harvey, ed. *Larousse Gastronomique.* New York: Crown Publishers, 1988.

Mariani, John F. *The Encyclopedia of American Food and Drink.* New York: Lebhar-Friedman, 1999.

Marshall, Lydie. *A Passion for Potatoes.* New York: Harper Perennial, 1992.

McGee, Harold. *On Food and Cooking.* New York: Charles Scribner's Sons, 1984.

Meyer, Nicole Aimée, and Amanda Pilar Smith. *Paris in a Basket.* Cologne, Germany: Konemann, 2000.

National Research Council. *Lost Crops of the Incas.* Washington, D.C.: National Academy Press, 1989.

Patraker, Joel, and Joan Schwartz. *The Greenmarket Cookbook.* New York: Viking, 2000.

Redon, Odile, Françoise Sabbam, and Silvano Serventi. *The Medieval Kitchen.* Chicago: University of Chicago Press, 1998.

Root, Waverley. *Food.* New York: Simon & Schuster, 1980.

Rozin, Elizabeth. *Blue Corn and Chocolate.* New York: Alfred A. Knopf, 1992.

Schneider, Elizabeth. *Uncommon Fruits and Vegetables: A Commonsense Guide*. New York: Harper & Row, 1986.

Spencer, Colin, and Claire Clifton, ed. *The Faber Book of Food*. Boston and London: Faber & Faber, 1993.

Tannahill, Reay. *Food in History*. New York: Crown Publishers, 1989.

Tihany, Adam, Francesco Antonucci, and Florence Fabricant. *Venetian Taste*. New York: Abbeville Press, 1994.

Toussaint-Samat, Maguelonne. *History of Food*. Translated by Anthea Bell. Cambridge, Mass.: Blackwell, 1992.

Trager, James. *The Food Book*. Old Tappan, N.Y.: Grossman Publishers, 1970.

_____. *The Food Chronology*. New York: Henry Holt, 1995.

Ward, Susie, Claire Clifton, and Jenny Stacey. *The Gourmet Atlas*. New York: Macmillan, 1997.

Wright, Clifford. *A Mediterranean Feast*. New York: William Morrow and Co., 1999.

Zuckerman, Larry. *The Potato*. New York: Faber & Faber 1998.

Index